The Ethics of Human Cloning

John Woodward, *Book Editor*

Bruce Glassman, *Vice President*
Bonnie Szumski, *Publisher*
Helen Cothran, *Managing Editor*

GREENHAVEN PRESS
An imprint of Thomson Gale, a part of The Thomson Corporation

Detroit • New York • San Francisco • San Diego • New Haven, Conn.
Waterville, Maine • London • Munich

For more information, contact
Greenhaven Press
27500 Drake Rd.
Farmington Hills, MI 48331-3535
Or you can visit our Internet site at http://www.gale.com

LIBRARY OF CONGRESS CATALOGING-IN-PUBLICATION DATA

The ethics of human cloning / John Woodward, book editor.
    p. cm. — (At issue)
Includes bibliographical references and index.
ISBN 0-7377-2186-3 (lib. bdg. : alk. paper) —
ISBN 0-7377-2187-1 (pbk. : alk. paper)
    1. Human cloning—Moral and ethical aspects. I. Woodward, John, 1958– .
II. At issue (San Diego, Calif.)
QH438.7.E844 2005
176—dc22   2004048217

Printed in the United States of America

Contents

Introduction

Science and religion have frequently been in conflict throughout much of human history, but human cloning may be uniquely controversial among scientific developments due to the powerful, fundamental questions it raises. It leads both the secular and the religious to reflect on the nature of humanity, the concept of self, and the meaning of life.

The views of the world's great religions on human cloning can have a profound impact on whether nations such as the United States eventually ban or legalize this controversial technology.

Judaism holds a fairly positive view of cloning. One of the fundamental tenets of Judaism is that God wants human beings to use all of their capacities to improve the health of others. In addition, Jewish law does not recognize the human embryo as a human being. Therefore, to the extent that therapeutic cloning, whereby scientists extract stem cells from embryos, could lead to cures for diseases, most Jewish scholars believe it should be allowed. The Union of Orthodox Jewish Congregations of America and the Rabbinical Council of America issued a policy statement on therapeutic cloning stating that because the procedure could lead to cures for devastating diseases, it should be allowed. "The Torah commands us to treat and cure the ill and to defeat disease wherever possible; to do this is to be the Creator's partner in safeguarding the created," they said. The council added: "The traditional Jewish perspective thus emphasizes that maximizing the potential to save and heal human life is an integral part of valuing human life." However, reproductive cloning, a procedure that produces a child, raises deep concerns in Jewish thought because of questions about how a clone would affect familial relationships. Some Jewish scholars worry that cloning could make human beings commodities by making it possible to breed clones to have certain characteristics, such as physical strength or high intelligence. The Rabbinical Council has affirmed its opposition to reproductive cloning.

Not all Jews disapprove of reproductive cloning, however.

Rabbi Michael Broyde expressed the view of some adherents to Reform Judaism when he argued in favor of reproductive cloning: "In sum, one is inclined to state that halacha (Jewish law and custom) views cloning as far less than the ideal way to reproduce people; however, when no other method is available it would appear that Jewish law accepts that having children through cloning is perhaps a mitzvah (blessing) in a number of circumstances and is morally neutral in a number of other circumstances."

There is no similar diversity of opinion in the Roman Catholic Church, which is adamantly opposed to any form of human cloning and has worked to mobilize political opposition to it. The official position of the church is that life begins at conception. In the church's view, creation of life and subsequent destruction of it for therapeutic or research purposes is equivalent to murder. In a speech to Vatican-based diplomats, Pope John Paul II expressed the official position of the Roman Catholic Church when he called the right to life "the most fundamental of human rights. Abortion, euthanasia, [and] human cloning . . . risk reducing the human person to a mere object. . . . When all moral criteria are removed, scientific research involving the sources of life becomes a denial of the being and the dignity of the person." He added: "These techniques, insofar as they involve the manipulation and destruction of human embryos, are not morally acceptable, even when their proposed goal is good in itself." Expressing a belief shared by adherents to most religions, he insisted that moral guidelines must always govern scientific inquiry: "What is technically possible is not for that reason alone morally admissible."

Similarly, Orthodox Christian churches, including the Russian Orthodox Church and the Greek Orthodox Church, see no situation in which cloning human beings would be acceptable. They see human reproductive cloning as an attempt to create human beings in man's image rather than God's. According to Father Vsevolod Chaplin, archpriest of the Russian Orthodox Church, "If human clones are bred for the egotistical reason of giving one person a second, a third, a hundred or more lives, then a profound moral crisis arises. . . . What sort of person would it be, knowing that he, of all people, was somebody's copy?" Reverend Demetrios Demopulos, parish priest of Holy Trinity Greek Orthodox Church and a holder of a PhD in genetics, writes, "As an Orthodox Christian, I speak out in opposition to any attempt to clone a human being because humans are supposed to be created by acts of love between two people, not through the manipulation of cells in acts that are ultimately about self-love."

Among Protestants there is a greater degree of disagreement. Clergy and congregants in conservative evangelical denominations tend to be closely aligned with the Roman Catholic Church on most social issues, and their views on cloning are no different. "Cloning is unethical and immoral and shows a complete disregard for the sanctity of human life," says conservative Presbyterian minister Dr. D. James Kennedy. Mainstream denominations, such as Methodists, generally disapprove of all forms of cloning, as well. In more liberal Protestant denominations, however, there is less uniformity of thought.

The denomination considered by many to be the most liberal of Protestant churches, the United Church of Christ, formed a committee on genetics that expressed mild support for therapeutic cloning up to the fourteenth day after conception—the approximate period when the beginnings of the nervous system can be detected in a human embryo. According to church doctrine, the United Church of Christ does not oppose "research that produces and studies cloned human pre-embryos through the 14th day of fetal development, provided the research is well justified in terms of its objectives, that the research protocols show proper respect for the pre-embryos, and that they not be implanted." The United Church of Christ General Synod passed a resolution in 2001 endorsing embryonic stem cell research that is conducted on embryos donated from fertility clinics. In 2001 Presbyterian Church (USA) General Assembly also issued a statement of support for embryonic stem cell research performed on embryos from in vitro fertilization clinics.

Despite their many differences with the West, most traditional Muslims also reject the idea of human cloning. Islam's holy book, the Koran, states that the creation of human beings results from the joining of the reproductive seeds of a husband and wife. Reproductive cloning, which bypasses this union, is therefore considered unnatural and in opposition to Islam. In 1983 the Islamic Organization for Medical Sciences (IOMS) convened a seminar on the Islamic view of human reproduction and determined that human cloning was not permissible. According to IOMS,

> Ordinary human cloning, in which the nucleus of
> a living somatic cell from an individual is placed

into the cytoplasm of an egg devoid of its nucleus, is not to be permitted. . . . All Muslim countries are called upon to formulate the necessary legislation to prevent foreign research institutes, organisations and experts from directly or indirectly using Muslim countries for experimentation on human cloning or promoting it.

For some Muslims, however, therapeutic cloning may be permissible because of their belief that the embryo does not have moral standing until 120 days after conception. This traditional belief is also shared by many Jews, and was accepted by most Christians until scientific advances in the nineteenth century allowed the microscopic visualization of sperm, eggs, and fertilization, which revealed nascent life.

In the Hindu world, objections to human cloning arise from a different religious tenet. All cloning research violates a fundamental principle of Hinduism: doing no harm to other creatures. Animal cloning experiments, during which a large percentage of the clones die prematurely or have serious birth defects, obviously violate this principle. Human cloning, many experts say, would involve the same failure rate. As a result, most Hindus reject all cloning, including animal cloning.

The only one of the world's great religions that appears to embrace all forms of human cloning, or at least is neutral about them, is Buddhism. In the Buddhist world view, the earth is a place of suffering in which sickness, old age, and death are unavoidable. The only way to be liberated from this world is through enlightenment, the state of full understanding of the nature of existence. The concept of individuality is alien to Buddhism, so Buddhist scholars generally believe that the way children are born is irrelevant. In fact, a few believe reproductive cloning might even be a method of reaching the state of enlightenment more quickly because the process could involve selectively breeding people with advanced moral qualities. Many Buddhists believe that therapeutic cloning may help to liberate people from the world of suffering. According to Professor Yong Moon of Korea's Seoul National University, "Cloning is a different way of thinking about the recycling of life. It's a Buddhist way of thinking."

As the debate about human cloning intensifies, many are looking to religious leaders for guidance. Others oppose the influence of religion on cloning decisions, pointing out that the

United States is officially a secular country. Yet in a nation that guarantees freedom of religion, most agree that diverse religious viewpoints can be helpful in informing many decisions in the public sphere, as long as those beliefs are part of a free and open discussion and are not ordained by the state.

The following viewpoints in *At Issue: The Ethics of Human Cloning* express some of the current thinking about the ethics of human cloning. From these arguments, it is clear that as the technology advances, passions on both sides of the debate will intensify. As scientists perfect cloning technology, there is no question that a variety of religious voices will increasingly shape the debate about human cloning.

1

The Ethics of Human Cloning: An Overview

Glenn McGee

Glenn McGee is associate director for education at the Center for Bioethics at the University of Pennsylvania School of Medicine's Center for Bioethics, as well as assistant professor of bioethics in the departments of philosophy, history, and sociology.

Human cloning involves implanting the DNA from one organism into an egg whose nucleus has been removed. After being artificially manipulated, the egg behaves as though fertilized and begins developing into a second organism with the same DNA as the first. Some argue that human cloning is repugnant; others see it as a valuable treatment for infertility. Some of the concerns about cloning center on the clone's physical well-being, as early human cloning attempts will likely lead to miscarriages, abortions, or deformed babies. Other concerns revolve around ethics; human cloning calls into question reproductive rights and the nature of the family.

Human somatic cell nuclear transfer, otherwise known (somewhat inaccurately) as creating an embryo by "cloning," involves:

- The starvation and subsequent implantation of DNA from specialized, non-sexual cells of one organism (e.g., cells specialized to make that organism's hair or milk) into an egg whose DNA nucleus has been removed.
- The resulting egg and nucleus are shocked or chemically treated so that the egg begins to behave as though fertil-

ization has occurred, resulting in the beginning of embryonic development of a second organism containing the entire genetic code of the first organism.

Mammalian cloning, through this nuclear transfer process, has resulted in the birth of hundreds of organisms to date. However, significantly more nuclear transfer generated embryos fail during pregnancy than would fail in sexual reproduction, and a substantial majority of cloned animals who have survived to birth have had some significant birth defect.

> *A child born as a genetic copy of another may feel undue pressure to become like or different from its progenitor.*

Reproduction, or perhaps more accurately, replication of an organism's DNA identity does not normally occur in mammals, with the exception of twinning, which always results in the simultaneous birth of siblings. Only plants reproduce through replication from one generation to another. The prospect of such replication for humans has resulted in the most controversial debate about reproduction ever to be taken up in western civilization.

In addition to the obvious risks to the first child, noted below, those who oppose human cloning point to the repugnance of a style of reproduction with such profound potential for vanity, arguing that the freedom of children and nature of the family are in danger.

Proponents of cloning suggested it might serve as a new, unusual but perhaps efficacious treatment for infertility, enabling those unable to pass genes to future generations to do so in a way that is at least analogous to the familial linkage of twins.

Perhaps the most urgent ethical, legal and social issues about cloning arise in the context and process that may lead to the birth of a first human clone. This is so because, as has been pointed out by scholars and politicians, early human experiments are likely to result in a number of clinical failures and lead to miscarriage, the necessity of dozens or even hundreds of abortions, or births of massively deformed offspring. Recent study of mammalian cloning also suggests that a number of defects often created in the reprogramming of the egg do not manifest themselves until later in the life of the resulting clone, so that mature clones have often undergone spectacular, unforeseen deaths.

The danger in cloning

The dangers for early prospective clones are controversial and difficult to manage because

- in part, one is attempting to protect a future potential person against harms that might be inflicted by their very existence, and
- in part because societies around the world have indicated that they believe that the early cloning experiments will breach a natural barrier that is moral in character, taking humans into a realm of self-engineering that vastly exceeds any prior experiments with new reproductive technology.

Laws that would prevent the birth of a first clone are difficult because they traverse complex jurisprudential ground: protecting an as-yet nonexistent life against reproductive dangers, in a western world that, in statutory and case law at least, favors reproductive autonomy.

Ethical concerns

But the dangers for the first clone pale in comparison to the ethical issues that will arise should cloning succeed in producing a healthy child, and become part of the repertoire of new reproductive technologies presently offered to those with sufficient funds.

- The creation of Dolly the sheep at Roslyn, Scotland labs of biotechnology company PPL Therapeutics (and not-for-profit Roslyn Institute) did not involve any of the hallmarks of what is known socially, religiously, and scientifically, as conception: the fusion of egg and sperm and the adhesion of the thus fertilized egg to the wall of the uterus.
- The genetic and cellular material that led to Dolly indeed might not even qualify in traditional terms as an embryo, in that mammalian embryos are scientifically defined in part by how they come into being. It is quite difficult to divine "what is in the dish" where a "clone" is being created, a problem that plagues all those who would define

and regulate the creation and research on embryonic progenitors of a clone.

By analogy, many have speculated as to whether

- a human clone lacks traits necessary for true independence from "parent" progenitors
- whether a clone is entitled by contrast to feel that a progenitor (genetically its monozygotic twin) is an appropriate parent
- and many in the general public in western nations identified the most important problem of cloning as whether a clone would have a soul.

How a clone is to be defined, or rather how difficult is the task of finding a way of understanding human cloning in terms from traditional language and contemporary institutions of science and parenting, has proven to be a most formidable challenge.

Implications for society

In moral terms, the questions to be asked about cloning, were it shown to be safe and effective, are:

- Whether and how does cloning relate to other kinds of families?
- What sorts of boundaries of parenthood and social responsibility are challenged by cloning?

Legal scholars have argued that cloning may violate, for example, a child's "right to an open future." A child born as a genetic copy of another may feel undue pressure to become like or different from its progenitor. Yet a right to an open future is difficult to validate by common law or analogy to ethical analysis about parenthood. What is parenthood, after all, but the teaching of values and knowledge to children in an act of stewardship? Perhaps children do not ever have fully open futures. Failing an absolute standard, society will have to find ways to reconcile differences among the many kinds and degrees of parental control and enhancement of children. While it is tempting to describe cloning as either a radical new form of parenting or as twinning, either analysis fails to take account of the need for new ways to integrate the problem of cloning into social institutions before it becomes an accepted form of reproductive medicine.

Cloning offers remarkable insight into the power of creation that humanity has taken into its fold. One theological analysis holds that humans are co-creators with God; perhaps it is more accurate to say that humans are moving ever closer to a posture of making babies, rather than having babies. Cloning represents a remarkable test of human restraint, wisdom and institutional development, one that will in many ways identify the moral features of 21st century biotechnology.

2

Reproductive Cloning Is Moral

Panayiotis Zavos

Panayiotis Zavos is a leading researcher and authority in the areas of male reproductive physiology, gamete physiology, male infertility, andrology, and other assisted reproductive technologies. Zavos is also an international authority on smoking and its effects on human reproductive performance.

In vitro fertilization (IVF) technology has allowed many infertile couples to have children, but for some, the only hope is reproductive regeneration, or human cloning. Passing laws against cloning will not prevent it from happening. The better solution is to regulate it and allow infertile couples to produce healthy, biologically related children with this technology. The political opponents of human cloning are making the same mistake that opponents of in vitro fertilization did in the 1970s. Despite their dire warnings, IVF has not resulted in adverse consequences but has, just as cloning will, helped desperate couples exercise their reproductive rights. We should forge ahead with this new technology.

Editor's Note: The following viewpoint was originally given as testimony before the House Subcommittee on Criminal Justice, Drug Policy, and Human Resources on May 15, 2002.

I am a Reproductive Specialist and Scientist that has dedicated the last 24 years of my life in helping infertile couples have children and complete their biological cycle. In January 2001, we have announced the possibility of using reproductive

Panayiotis Zavos, testimony before the House Subcommittee on Criminal Justice, Drug Policy, and Human Resources, Washington, DC, May 15, 2002.

regeneration technologies as a means of treating infertility, and our intention to develop these technologies in a safe and responsible manner. However, we have received great opposition from fellow scientists, news media and the general public. It seems that the great opposition is due to the lack of complete understanding and comprehension of what in actuality human cloning really is all about. The British Medical Association however, has so appropriately stated: "Public hostility to human reproductive cloning may be based on an illogical transient fear of a new technology". Much of the confusion is caused by the variance in opinions coming from different scientific sources, politicians, news media and Hollywood. Due to the limited knowledge of these technological and medical procedures in the Scientific Community, we have organized, hosted and attended meetings involving scientists from all over the world to discuss and debate the issues of human reproductive regeneration. We have even presented our intentions before the Congress of the United States last year [2001].

The problem of infertility

Infertility affects approximately 10–15% of couples of reproductive age throughout the developing world. Assisted Reproductive Technologies (ART) have played a major role in treating various causes of infertility. In fact, about 65% of the couples who seek medical help will eventually succeed in having a child. However, in cases where there are no sperm or eggs present (possibly due to loss of testicular or ovarian function), the only options these couples face are sperm donation, oocyte donation or adoption. These are difficult choices for couples to make and many do not want to use sperm or egg sources other than their own or do not wish to consider adoption. Reproductive regeneration (RR), which is synonymous to reproductive cloning, can therefore play a very real role in the treatment of severe male or female infertility in couples that wish to have their own biological children.

After a lot of time, money and suffering, many of the infertile couples have been able to have children using present IVF [in vitro fertilization] techniques. Personally, it has given me great satisfaction to assist them in the creation of their own families. However, some of these infertile couples have not been able to experience the joy of creating their own families because the present technologies are not advanced enough to help them. For them, human reproductive cloning is the only way they can have their own children. As a Reproductive Specialist and a scientist who cares about their plight, I am trying to develop safe techniques of human cloning so they can have the healthy babies they want. Mr. Chairman, am I wrong in wanting to help couples become parents?

> *It seems that the great opposition is due to the lack of complete understanding and comprehension of what in actuality human cloning really is all about.*

If you care about these unfortunate infertile couples, why are you considering legislation that would make both them and the people that are trying to help them, criminals? Criminalizing human reproductive cloning in the United States will only make it less safe and more costly for these infertile couples. They will be forced to travel outside the United States to pursue their dream of creating a family. After all, according to the Americans with Disabilities Act (ADA), infertility is a disability and reproduction is a major life activity for the purposes of the ADA (*Bragdon v. Abbott*, 118 S.Ct 2196; 1998). In light of this, it is the right of each and every American citizen to bear a child.

Cloning cannot be prevented

Mr. Chairman, experts state repeatedly that history proves the point very clearly that scientists will clone even if President [George W.] Bush and the Congress forbid it. The House of Representatives may vote against human cloning but that will not stop scientists from doing it and people from wanting it. The American Society for Reproductive Medicine (ASRM) of which I am a long standing member, recently stated that "thousands of years of human experience have shown us that governments cannot bottle up human progress, even when you want to" and that "there is every reason to believe that if passed, this kind of prohibition would not be effective". In another case made by a infertility patient, who wants her own genetic baby so badly that she would go wherever she had to, in order to clone either herself or her husband "if they called me right now and said, 'We're paying for everything and giving you the chance to have your own genetic child,' I would be on a plane so fast it's not even funny," she said. In the words of a bioethicist "The best way to control this research is to fund it by the federal government, because then you create rules," and in my words Mr. Chairman, this Genie is out of the bottle and it keeps getting bigger by the hour. There is no way that this Genie is going back into the bottle. Let us find ways to develop it properly and disseminate it safely.

Banning human reproductive cloning in the United States will not stop human cloning. In fact, the first cloned pregnancy may have occurred already. If you institute a ban, all that will happen is exactly what happened when the first IVF baby was born in 1978. The United States banned IVF when it first came out and then after several years, decided it had made a mistake and spent the next several years catching up with the technology that was advanced in other countries. The only people that suffered were the infertile U.S. couples who were unable to have children or had to travel outside of the United States to receive these treatments. Let us show the proper compassion for those suffering American infertile couples. Let us give them some hope and let us not turn our backs on them. They deserve something better than that.

> *Criminalizing human reproductive cloning in the United States will only make it less safe and more costly for these infertile couples.*

If you are concerned about the risks of human cloning, the proper approach is to fund it and then institute regulations that will insure that human cloning is done properly with a minimum of risk for the baby just as is done in other medical or drug innovations. This is what our team is working on and we will not go forward with human cloning until the risks are comparable with other IVF procedures. Of course, because of the present political climate in the United States, we have been forced to look elsewhere in the world for a proper venue. We have no intentions of doing this in the USA whether any legislation is passed for or against this technology. Furthermore, Mr. Chairman, we have no intentions of breaking the laws of this country or any other country to accomplish this. We are law abiding citizens of this great Nation of ours, but we are a compassionate group of people that wish to help our fellow man and woman have the gift of life. The gift of life that most of us have been so fortunate to have, enjoy and take for granted. Let us not be so uncompassionate and so insensitive to tell those people that we are not willing to listen to them and unwilling to help them. This is not what our Country's constitution and principles are based on. We believe in creating families, not preventing them. In God we trust!

Reproductive regeneration as an infertility treatment

The incidence of developmental abnormalities following natural sexual reproduction in humans is 3% and is significantly higher when maternal age is over 40. As recently reported in the *New England Journal of Medicine*, the risks are even greater from IVF and other more advanced ART procedures yielding more than 30,000 children per year in the USA. It is vividly clear that thousands of potential parents accept these risks to conceive a child. If human reproductive regeneration is banned as a reproductive technique on safety grounds, then we may find ourselves in the untenable position of having banned all reproductive techniques which suffer equal or higher risks, thereby, possibly even banning natural sexual reproduction with its 3% risk, a situation that the majority of people would consider ridiculous. It appears reasonable to suggest that the incidence of developmental abnormalities as to the safety of human reproductive regeneration is negligible when compared to current risks associated with IVF and other ART procedures.

> *There is no way that this Genie is going back into the bottle. Let us find ways to develop it properly and disseminate it safely.*

It is quite evident to us along with other competent human reproductive specialists that with further elucidation of the molecular mechanisms involved during the processes of embryogenesis, careful tailoring of subsequently developed culture conditions and manipulation strategies, and appropriate screening methods, will eventually allow infertile couples to safely have healthy, genetically related children through SCNT [Somatic Cell Nuclear Transfer] methods.

The opponents of human cloning

The most prominent opponents to human reproductive regeneration and spokesmen for animal cloning are Drs. Ian Wilmut from the Roslin Institute and Rudolph Jaenisch from the Massachusetts Institute of Technology (MIT), who have misled and have misdirected the public and its leadership for their very own gains, whatever those gains might be. They have repeatedly stated that the application of animal cloning technologies to humans, is extremely dangerous, not because of ethical and social implications, but because of the foreseeable possibility that cloning humans might result in a very high incidence of developmental abnormalities, large offspring syndrome (LOS), placental malfunctions, respiratory distress and circulatory problems, the most common causes of neonatal death in animals. They also noted that the rate of success as an ART method is extremely low, being only 3%. Furthermore, they state that because since the production of Dolly the sheep in 1995, they have not improved on these technologies themselves, they have concluded that reproductive regeneration is not safe and efficient for use in humans, and would like for the world to believe this. Let us examine the facts as they appear.

> *Let us show the proper compassion for those suffering American infertile couples. Let us give them some hope and let us not turn our backs on them. They deserve something better than that.*

If one reviews the animal cloning literature, one can deduce that the poor cloning success rates noted by the "animal cloners" are mainly due to experiments that were (i) poorly designed, (ii) poorly executed, (iii) poorly approached, and (iv) poorly understood and interpreted. These experiments were mostly done under non-sterile and uncontrolled environments and having a "hit-and-miss" type of outcome. Also, when the cloned animals died, no clear view of their cause of death was ascertained. In short, their experimentation methods lacked the seriousness of purpose that is vital when performing similar studies in humans. Furthermore, the same scientists responsible for Dolly, the sheep, now plan to utilize similar crude technologies to experiment on cloned human embryos for medical purposes.

According to a recent article in *Time* magazine, Wilmut and Jaenisch stated "animal cloning is inefficient and is likely to remain so for the foreseeable future". On the contrary, a number of studies have already demonstrated far higher rates of success and, in some cases, matching or exceeding successes noted in human IVF today. Also, if history is any indicator, one can reasonably expect that further refinements to the cloning process will improve efficiency rates. Scientists have reported success rates of 32% in goats and 80% in cows since 1998, as opposed to the poor 3% success rate Wilmut obtained when cloning Dolly in 1995. Furthermore, scientists at Advanced Cell Technologies in Worcester, Massachusetts, in association with others, have recently produced 24 cloned cows, that were all normal and healthy and have survived to adulthood. Despite the overwhelming data that exists showing refinements in the RR technology that yield improving success rates, Wilmut and Jaenisch still insist that it is inefficient based upon their poor success using very crude and uncontrolled experimental techniques, almost seven years ago. One can only but question their motives for their illogical arguments. They do not seem interested in developing and refining techniques, but they rather seem to have immense private interests and want to patent and control the technologies for themselves. Interestingly enough, the Roslin Institute scientists who cloned Dolly the sheep have changed their agenda on the cloning subject and have stated recently that they plan to seek permission to experiment on cloned human embryos for medical purposes. What are their true motives?

Animal cloning vs. human cloning

It has been very clearly shown that animal cloning and its difficulties appear to be species-specific, and the data cannot be extrapolated with a great degree of accuracy to the human species. In a recent study by scientists from Duke University Medical Center, it was demonstrated that it may be technically easier and safer to perform somatic cell nuclear transfer (SCNT) in humans than in sheep cows, pigs, and mice because humans possess a genetic benefit that prevents fetal overgrowth, one of the major obstacles encountered in cloning animals.

The genetic benefit is based on the fact that humans and other primates possess two activated copies of a gene called insulin like growth factor II receptor (IGF2R). Offspring receive one functional copy from each parent as expected. However sheep, pigs, mice and virtually all non-primate mammals receive only one functional copy of this gene because of a rare phenomenon known as genomic imprinting in which the gene is literally stamped with marking that turn off its function. Since humans are not imprinted at IGF2R, then fetal overgrowth would not be predicted to occur if humans were cloned. If this theory is correct, the incidence of developmental abnormalities following human SCNT would be significantly lower. Also, the authors concluded that the data showed that one does not necessarily have these problems in humans. This is the first concrete genetic data showing that the cloning process could be less complicated in humans than in sheep.

The political status of cloning

In the United States, the House passed in July, 2001 the Weldon Bill or the Human Cloning Prohibition Act of 2001 (bill H.R. 2505). This bill would prohibit any person or entity, in or affecting interstate commerce, from (i) performing or attempting to perform human cloning, (ii) participating in such an attempt, (iii) shipping or receiving the product of human cloning, or (iv) importing such a product. The bill currently pending in the US Senate, S 790, written by Sen. Sam Brownback (R Kansas), would criminalize all cloning with a fine of up to $1 million and 10 years in prison and it is almost identical to the bill (H.R. 2505) passed by the House in July 2001. The Council of Europe has introduced a protocol that prevents any abuses of such techniques by applying them to humans, banning "any intervention seeking to create a human being genetically identical to another human being, whether living or dead". Finally, the Protocol leaves it to countries' domestic law to define the scope of the term "human being". In April 24, 2001, England has banned "reproductive regeneration" but not "therapeutic cloning".

The political situation with cloning in general remains very fluid, mainly because of the inability of the politicians to understand, comprehend and act decisively on the issues that cloning presents to society. After all, their inability to act decisively may have a great deal to do with their resistance to debate and face the facts that humans will be cloned.

In his speech to the American public, President Bush made an appeal for a global ban on cloning, whether it be for therapeutic or reproductive cloning, on the basis that we should not use people for "spare parts" and we should not "manufacture people". Reproductive cloning does neither. As opposed to therapeutic cloning which results in the inevitable death of an embryo once the stem cells have been removed, reproductive cloning aims to protect and preserve life in allowing the embryo to grow and be implanted into the uterus for a subsequent pregnancy. From an ethical point of view, there is no destruction of life.

> *Reproductive cloning is nothing more than another modality for the treatment of human infertility in giving the gift of life to a childless couple.*

Quoting President Bush: "Life is a creation, not a commodity. Our children are gifts to be loved and protected, not products to be designed and manufactured. Allowing cloning would be taking a significant step toward a society in which human beings are grown for spare body parts, and children are engineered to custom specifications; and that's not acceptable." And that's not acceptable to us either, Mr. Chairman! We agree with President Bush and uphold the sanctity of human life. Reproductive cloning does not involve the destruction of human embryos, nor does it modify or "engineer" the genetic code to custom specifications. Reproductive cloning involves employment of similar technology used for Intra cytoplasmic Sperm Injection (ICSI), which is routinely employed in IVF centers throughout the World. The only difference is that instead of using a sperm cell from the father, scientists can use a somatic cell nucleus and inject it into the mother's anucleated egg. The resulting embryo would have its genetic makeup from the father, but the expression of the genetic code and characteristics and personality of the baby born will be completely different and unique. Reproductive cloning is nothing more than another modality for the treatment of human infertility in giving the gift of life to a childless couple that have exhausted all other choices for having a child. What is so wrong about this?

Is history repeating itself?

This is not the first time that the scientific community has had to deal with controversial issues regarding new technologies. Exactly the same events happened with IVF in the Kennedy Institute in Washington in 1978. Professor Robert Edwards and Dr. Patrick Steptoe were faced with such criticism from hundreds of reporters, senators, judges, scientists and doctors, when they proposed the idea of in-vitro fertilization. The language and accusations were the same as what we face today, including "they ignored the sanctity of life, performed immoral experiments on the unborn", "subject to absolute moral prohibition", "no certainty that the baby won't be born without defect" and to "accept the necessity of infanticide. There are going to be a lot of mistakes."

Twenty-four years later, the exact opposite of everything the "experts" predicted happened. IVF has become an acceptable and routine treatment of infertility worldwide. The abnormalities that were expected to have been unacceptable proved to be the same, if not less than with natural conception. Ironically, those critics of IVF have become the "pioneers" of IVF. These same critics might have delayed the introduction of IVF but their actions mostly harmed patients, and also the medical and scientific community. I am certain that the reproductive cloning procedures will follow in the same footsteps. Recently, I have had the opportunity to openly debate Professor Robert Winston from the UK, on the issue of human reproductive cloning at an Oxford Union Debate at Oxford University. Ironically enough, he was one of the leaders originally opposed to IVF, and who is currently a leading IVF specialist in Britain. The technology that he was vehemently opposed to, almost twenty-five years ago, is now the very same technology that he uses to earn a living. Once reproductive regeneration is commonplace in the ART treatment market, will he, along with all the other critics, "jump" on the bandwagon and offer this new technology in their own IVF centers? I believe so. They have done it before and they can do it again. Mr. Chairman, we can not afford to behave this way and most importantly wish to repeat the same mistake.

Cloning should be permitted

As Professor Robert Edwards, the great English scientist who helped create the world's first test-tube baby in 1978, so eloquently prophesied recently "Cloning, too, will probably come to be accepted as a reproductive tool if it is carefully controlled." No doubt, humans will be produced via reproductive regeneration. Recent scientific and technological progress demonstrates that very clearly. Similar to IVF, the technology of reproductive regeneration will advance, techniques will be improved, and knowledge will be gained. Reproductive regeneration's difficult questions can be answered only through a dedicated pursuit of knowledge and an exercise of our willful rationality, and in the end, the answer to the debate over human nature may be simply that man's nature is the product of his own will.

Mr. Chairman, science has been very good to us and we should not abandon it now. Consider why America has the best medical care in the world. It is because we have the freedom to investigate, research and market the latest medical techniques, all within proper procedures and safeguards. This is not the time to panic and try to turn back the clock. The Genie is already out of the bottle. Let's make sure it works for us, not against us. Let's do it here. Let's do it right. By banning cloning, America will be showing the world that she is hesitant and/or reluctant to take the lead in this new arena of technological advancement. The world today is looking at the most powerful nation on Earth for leadership on this issue, and walking away from it by banning it is not a sign of leadership, but cowardice. Do not let the future of this technology slip away through our fingers, because we are too afraid to embrace it. I believe that it is the right of the American people to choose whether or not they want to have this technology available to them. Let us educate ourselves and debate the issues and not make irrational decisions based upon fear of a new technology. Banning this technology would only give our enemies license to use it to their advantage. Let us learn from history and forge ahead in this brave new world as leaders, not spectators, the American way.

3

Reproductive Cloning Is Immoral

Economist

The Economist *is a weekly magazine of business and politics.*

Although mammals have been cloned successfully, the process is still mysterious and riddled with problems. Attempts to clone humans would certainly involve stillbirths and sudden deaths. In animal cloning, for example, for every one hundred eggs used, one resulting clone is considered a success. Fetuses that are aborted are frequently abnormally large or have other deformities. Moreover, half the seemingly normal cloned cows and sheep die within three weeks. Many problems and uncertainties still plague cloning efforts, which calls into question the morality of cloning humans.

Science fiction has not, on the whole, been kind to those at the cutting edge of human reproduction. From "Boys from Brazil" to "The 6th Day", Arnold Schwarzenegger's latest oeuvre, people in the awkward business of human cloning appear as crazed, power-hungry, profit-seeking individuals on the fringes of society.

On March 9th [2001], life took a turn towards art as a band of controversial scientists gathered before a mob of journalists in Rome to launch a project to produce a human by cloning. The protagonists—led by Severino Antinori, an Italian infertility specialist, Panos Zavos, an American researcher in the same area, and Avi Ben Abraham, an Israeli biotechnologist—plan to start tinkering with cells in the laboratory by the end of [March

2001] and to have a human clone alive and kicking by 2003.[1] They claim their aim is to tackle male infertility by allowing those not up to the job of old-fashioned or even test-tube fertilisation, to have children who share their genes.

> **❝** *The team's flamboyant scheme, which is long on secrecy but short on substance, has been condemned from all quarters and on a variety of counts.* **❞**

The team's flamboyant scheme, which is long on secrecy but short on substance, has been condemned from all quarters and on a variety of counts. Many oppose the whole notion of cloning humans as an affront to human dignity. Bioethicists are troubled by concerns for the clone's welfare, the viability of his or her family and the implications for wider society. Lawyers fret about the legality of such science, given regulations governing human cloning and embryo research in various countries. More surprisingly, strong arguments against the initiative come not just from those opposed to the principle of reproductive cloning, but also from researchers at the forefront of the technology.

Problems in animal cloning

Veterans, such as Alan Trounson at Monash University in Melbourne, Australia, have succeeded in cloning several species of mammal. But they are appalled at the prospect of trying the technique in humans when its problems have yet to be worked out in experimental animals. Dr Trounson, like many leading practitioners, is certain that human cloning can and will be done. Some of his colleagues, indeed, look forward to that day. What worries them is not the end, a cloned baby. Rather, they have serious doubts about the means, which will involve stillbirths and sudden deaths for as long as cloning remains a mysterious process.

Conventional fertilisation, in which sperm meets egg, is a complex event that brings together two half-sets of genetic ma-

---

1. Their efforts had not been successful when this volume went to press.

terial—one from each parent—to provide the resulting individual with a full complement of chromosomes. Cloning bypasses this by putting the genetic material from a pre-existing adult cell (which already carries a full complement of chromosomes) into an egg that has had its half-set of chromosomes removed. If all goes well, the egg will then develop into a normal, healthy individual.

Unfortunately, all seldom goes well. Naturally formed embryonic nuclei have the advantage of being new to the world. They are therefore adapted to the task of turning on the genes necessary for development. The nuclei of adult cells, in contrast, have settled into a quiet middle age. In them, most of the genes for early development have been turned off and are difficult to reinvigorate. The great leap forward in cloning came when Ian Wilmut and his colleagues at the Roslin Institute, near Edinburgh, found a way to awaken these sluggish nuclei. They produced a lively and, to all intents and purposes, normal sheep, known as Dolly, from the nucleus of a mammary-gland cell.

> *For every 100 eggs used, a researcher is lucky to end up with a single cloned calf or a solitary pig in a poke.*

Even so, according to Alan Colman, a nuclear transfer expert at PPL Therapeutics, a British biotechnology firm, cloning is still a crude process. For every 100 eggs used, a researcher is lucky to end up with a single cloned calf or a solitary pig in a poke. By comparison, in vitro fertilisation (IVF) has a success rate of roughly 25%.

The difference lies in the large number of individuals that fall by the wayside at every step of the cloning process. This begins with a stimulus, such as an electric shock, that promotes the fusion of an egg cell that has had its nucleus removed with a donor cell whose nucleus it will assume. Roughly four-fifths of fusions succeed, but only two-thirds start down the path of development that leads to a new individual.

After a couple of days, the newly nucleated cell should have divided to form a ball of cells called a blastocyst. Here again, losses occur, and only 10% of the original egg cells used in nuclear transfer make it this far. Once the blastocyst is implanted in the womb, at most 20% of pregnancies are carried to term, compared with three-fifths in IVF. The fetuses that are spontaneously aborted are often abnormally large. They also tend to have severe deformities, and their placentas are distorted. Finally, and most disturbingly to Dr Colman, half the cloned (and seemingly normal) cows and sheep that make it through to birth drop dead within three weeks. Post-mortem examination often reveals subtle, but nonetheless fatal, flaws in the heart muscle or kidneys of these animals—the sorts of changes that are hard to predict and therefore almost impossible to prevent.

Mysteries of reproduction

Researchers are only beginning to get a sense of the range of things that can go awry in cloning. Certainly, something unusual is happening in the process by which the egg cell sends out signals to reprogram its new nucleus and put the developmental genes back into action. There appears, in particular, to be a problem with a phenomenon known as genetic imprinting.

Most genes in a cell are present as two copies, one from the mother and one from the father. Imprinting is the process by which one of those copies is silenced so as not to overdose a cell with whatever that gene provides. Although the transplanted nucleus enters the egg properly imprinted, reprogramming messes this up. As a result, some genes become too active and others fail to work at all. By studying the expression patterns of individual genes, cloners have found that certain genes which should be turned on in early development, such as those that control the implantation of the embryo into the uterus, are activated much later in cloned embryos.

Unfortunately, they have little idea why this is the case. Nor do they know the full set of genes that go awry, which makes foolproof screening of faulty embryos impossible. Without such safeguards in place, there is no reason to assume that human cloning will not repeat the messy trial and error of current animal research. Not surprisingly, those who know reproductive cloning best are urging others to refrain from trying it on people until the bugs have been worked out on hundreds more animals.

Rushing to clone

Such uncertainties do not deter Dr Antinori and his crew. They believe the technical problems associated with animal cloning have been greatly exaggerated, and may not be relevant to humans. In any case, they reckon that their experience with IVF gives them "enough knowledge and sophistication and technology to break the rules of nature, and now is the time."

Dr Antinori is certainly well known in IVF circles, but more for such stunts as impregnating a 62-year-old woman using IVF than for his scientific prowess. In any case, success at IVF—which was thoroughly tested on animals before moving into humans and was never plagued by the sorts of trouble seen in nuclear transfer—is no guide to success in cloning. As yet, the team has little expertise in nuclear transfer, and although its members say they will try to bring the right people on board, the best in the business are unlikely to be drawn in while human reproductive cloning remains at the margins of scientific and social respectability.

As to cost, Dr Trounson estimates that it will take at least $1m to clone a human, given the equipment, labour and hundreds of human eggs that will be required to get a single, live birth. There are enough infertile couples desperate to reproduce, enough small sects eager to keep their numbers up and their gene pools pure, and enough megalomaniacs intent on replicating themselves, to make money the least of would-be cloners' problems. Indeed, Dr Zavos claims the consortium has more than enough cash to do its work, and up to 700 volunteers ready to take part. Few scientists believe that the group will reach its goal within the next two years, but many acknowledge that the technology will one day permit human reproductive cloning. Whether society will condone it is an entirely different matter.

4

Therapeutic Cloning Can Save Lives

Raymond Barglow

Raymond Barglow is a psychologist and a political activist.

Banning therapeutic cloning would block research that could lead to cures for many diseases. In therapeutic cloning, genetic material from an adult cell is placed inside an egg to grow beneficial stem cells, not to produce a baby. Therapeutic cloning would allow a patient's own genetic material to be used to repair his or her damaged cells. There is broad consensus in the scientific community that therapeutic cloning could lead to remedies for diseases such as Alzheimer's and cancer. It should be legal and regulated.

In his essay, "Why I Oppose Human Cloning," Jeremy Rifkin proposes that his view is widely shared within the progressive community: "many of us in the progressive left are equally opposed to both therapeutic and full birth cloning. . . . Earlier this year, sixty-seven leading progressives lent their support to legislation that would outlaw therapeutic and full birth cloning. The signatories of the anti-cloning petition included many of the best-known intellectuals and activists in left circles today." In fact, the petition came from Mr. Rifkin himself (the document became known as "the Rifkin petition"), and two of the petition's signers, Stanley Aronowitz and Quentin Young, have since withdrawn their support from the petition.

Some of Jeremy Rifkin's criticisms of reproductive cloning are well taken; I do not have the space here to discuss his argument in detail. But his campaign against therapeutic cloning (known by scientists as Somatic Cell Nuclear Transfer, or SCNT, which is explained below) is not equally justified.

In the domain of biomedicine, progressives can readily identify with Rifkin's opposition to "efforts to reduce human life and its various parts and processes to the status of mere research tools, manufactured products, and utilities." But despite his assertions to the contrary, few among us can see the link he assumes between the research cloning of embryonic stems cells for therapeutic purposes and the larger doomsday scenario that he lays out. The stem cell issue—which is receiving a lot of attention from the national media—has provided Rifkin with a wedge for introducing his anti-biotechnology agenda to a wide audience at the cost of neglecting the specific intentions and prospects of scientists working with embryonic stem cells to better understand disease processes and to develop new therapies based on that understanding.

The religious right

In its campaign to discredit embryonic stem cell research, the religious right has blurred the differences between therapeutic and reproductive cloning, creating in the popular imagination nightmare visions of cloned babies born into brave new worlds (evoked as well in popular entertainment like the movie *Attack of the Clones*). But therapeutic cloning provides scant supplies for these science fiction scenarios. This research is already subject to federal regulation, does not involve significant health risks to cell donors, does not alter existing genomes, and takes place in a laboratory setting with a handful of embryonic stem cells that will not be implanted in a womb.

Our task as progressives should be to expose the way that anti-abortion spokespersons twist the facts about this kind of research. Instead, Rifkin has allied himself with these very forces. He rightly points out that biomedical research needs careful ethical evaluation. And in his book *The Biotech Century*, he elaborated a fairly reasonable dialectical approach to such research, recognizing its enormous potential for good, while pointing out also the dangers. But now his blanket opposition to the cloning of human embryos abandons that balance in favor of dubious assumptions and misleading arguments. Banning therapeutic cloning would obstruct research paths that could lead to effective remedies for major illnesses such as childhood leukemia, diabetes, Alzheimer's, and Parkinson's disease.

Rifkin argues that "By concentrating research almost exclusively on magic bullets in the form of gene replacements, the medical community forecloses the less invasive option of prevention. . . ." This is erroneous on two counts. First, it overlooks what may be the most valuable result of research cloning: A better understanding of disease processes. Researchers can take a diseased cell from an adult (the disease in question could be cancer, cardiovascular disease, Alzheimer's, or another disease in which genetic inheritance or mutation plays a role) and use embryonic cloning to create a stem cell line from it. (The line's originating cells are harvested from the cloned embryo.) Studying a stem cell line of this kind—seeing how the disease develops as the stem cells differentiate—will help us understand that development and find remedies for it. For example, the way in which embryonic stem cells, which have been cloned using adult cells from an Alzheimer's patient, differentiate into brain cells can be compared with the normal formation of brain cells, thereby providing new information that might help us cure this disease. If SCNT research is criminalized, this entire domain of investigation will be shut down.

> *Our task as progressives should be to expose the way that anti-abortion spokespersons twist the facts about this kind of research.*

Second, research of this kind needn't be counterpoised to preventive measures (which indeed should be medicine's highest priority, as I've argued in an essay published in *Tikkun* March/April 2002). Consider diabetes for instance. Certainly we need to address the social/environmental factors that may be contributing to its increase over the past two decades. But anyone who has seen a child suffering from diabetes surely hopes also that a medical remedy will be found.

Regulation of complex technologies

Rifkin is right, however, to ask basic questions about the priorities and governance of biomedical research. Stem cell experimentation, for example, is a complex, multifaceted enterprise that advances at the cutting edge of scientific understanding.

How can it be made to conform to democratically-arrived-at norms of social responsibility? How can lay persons, lacking expertise in specialized scientific/technological domains, intelligently evaluate the research approaches that scientists come up with?

Progressives have faced this quandary many times before—in our opposition to the nuclear power industry, for instance. In arriving at our judgments about the advisability of using complex technologies, we rely a lot upon the views of authorities who are respected within progressive/environmentalist circles—upon "our" experts, whom we take to be more conscientious and less aligned with profit-seeking interests than are the advocates on "the other side."

> *Many debilitating medical conditions are caused by cell damage. Therapeutic cloning . . . could allow a patient's own genetic material to be used to repair that damage.*

In the domain of biotechnology, which deploys methods of cellular and molecular investigation that most of us know little or nothing about, how are we to figure out which pathways are ethically and politically acceptable? We may accept the guidance of people like Jeremy Rifkin who have considerable specialized knowledge. Rifkin himself would probably agree, however, that we cannot blindly trust the "experts," even when they espouse values that we believe in.

Here are responses to some of the questions that have been raised about therapeutic cloning research:

Why we need therapeutic cloning

The diagram labeled "Research Cloning" illustrates the crucial differences between two kinds of cloning: therapeutic and reproductive. Therapeutic cloning places the genetic material from an adult cell inside an egg, in order to grow therapeutically beneficial stem cells, not to produce a baby. These cells can be used in scientific research to deepen our comprehension of disease origins and development, and to develop new medical therapies.

Many debilitating medical conditions are caused by cell damage. Therapeutic cloning (SCNT), could allow a patient's own genetic material to be used to repair that damage. Replacement cells—neurons, blood cells, pancreatic cells, etc.—generated from cloned stem cells would be much less likely to be rejected by a patient's immune system, since they would be genetically identical to the debilitated tissue they were replacing.

Forty Nobel Laureates recently issued a statement that finds this research promising. They cite the prospect of developing cell-replacement therapies, and also of advancing our understanding of fundamental disease processes: "it may be possible to use nuclear transplantation technology to produce patient-specific embryonic stem cells that could overcome the rejection normally associated with tissue and organ transplantation. Nuclear transplantation technology might also permit the creation of embryonic stem cells with defined genetic constitution, permitting a new and powerful approach to understanding how inherited predispositions lead to a variety of cancers and neurological diseases such as Parkinson's and Alzheimer's diseases."

Among biomedical researchers in the United States, there is a broad consensus that the research cloning of embryonic stem cells may lead to new remedies for severe childhood and adult illnesses that afflict millions of people. On February 8 of this year [2002], the National Academy of Sciences concluded that therapeutic cloning "offers great promise for treating diseases. . . . Closing these avenues of research may have real costs for millions of people who now have these diseases."

Embryonic stem cells

Rifkin suggests that "few, if any, on the left oppose research on adult stem cells, which can be taken from individuals after birth and have proved promising in both animal studies and clinical trials. This 'soft path' approach poses none of the ethical, social, and economic risks of strategies using embryo stem cells." Most scientists working in this area, however, believe that adult stem cells are less promising for research purposes than embryonic ones. Embryonic stem cells haven't been damaged by aging, and they show a much greater plasticity—the potential for developing into a variety of specialized cells that could be used in life-saving therapies—than adult ones do. Two recent studies published in *Nature* (March 13, 2002), one of them conducted at the University of Florida and the other by researchers at the University of Edinburgh, cast doubt on previous claims that adult stem cells could revert to an earlier stage of development. In any event, researchers in this domain need to study and work with both embryonic and adult stem cells. We do not yet know which particular path of investigation will lead to useful therapies.

There is an additional and very important use of cloned embryonic stem cells in medical research that adult stem cells cannot serve. As explained above, stem cell lines that result from the embryonic cloning of diseased cells can help us better understand the inception and development of major diseases.

> *If a person can agree to participate, for example, in a dangerous malaria vaccine study to help prevent or cure this disease, why should she be prevented from donating eggs for similar (but much safer) lifesaving research?*

Will therapeutic cloning inevitably lead us onto a slippery slope to the production of cloned human babies? No. Federal authority can make it illegal to implant a cloned embryo into a uterus. Our model for regulatory oversight should be the English Fertilisation and Embryology Act of 1990, which limits any experimentation with embryos to the first fourteen days. It is at fourteen days that an embryo first begins to develop the primitive streak, the first indication of a nervous system. It is also at fourteen days that, in all but the most extreme case, an embryo loses the ability to split into two and become twins. The oversight mandated by the English Act has prevented any "slippery slope" in the United Kingdom and there is no reason to assume that a similar approach would not work as well in this country.

Will therapeutic cloning lead to unethical incentives being offered for women's eggs, as Rifkin suggests? The prospect of an increased market for women's eggs is a legitimate concern. But our aim should be to regulate, not to criminalize, the procedures whereby scientists obtain egg cells for research purposes. Moreover, there are clearly some cases where the concern for improper incentives or risk of egg donation would not be relevant—when a mother wishes to donate an egg to help her child, for example, or to create stem cells that could be used to save her own life. If a person can agree to participate, for example, in a dangerous malaria vaccine study to help prevent or cure this disease, why should she be prevented from donating eggs for similar (but much safer) lifesaving research?

Cloning should be regulated

All of the constituencies that have a stake in the benefits of this research need to devise effective regulations for its continuation. We agree with Jeremy Rifkin that we ought not to trust blindly the scientific community or biotech industry. Legislative bodies—with the participation of scientists, medical practitioners, patients' groups, and other interested parties—need to improve already existing statutes regarding egg donation for any purpose: in vitro fertilization, surrogate motherhood, or therapeutic cloning. This is the democratic way to address the relevant social and ethical concerns.

It is also important to note that by researching therapeutic cloning, scientists hope to understand the biological properties of a cloned egg cell that induce it to generate stem cells. Once they learn how this cell "re-programming" occurs, they may no longer need to use egg cells.

Irving Weissman, a biology professor at Stanford, compares the current debate over stem cell research to the 1970s controversy over recombinant DNA technology, which now produces a broad range of medicines, including cancer and diabetes treatments. He points out that "the lives of hundreds of thousands of Americans each year are saved or made better by such recombinant DNA products. . . . I believe the kind of medical research that can follow from nuclear transplantation will have a similar magnitude of medical benefits."

Because of its therapeutic potential, research that clones stem cells for medical purposes deserves our support. It should be publicly funded and better regulated, not outlawed.

5

Therapeutic Cloning Is Immoral

William Saunders

William Saunders is senior fellow in human life studies at the Family Research Council, a public policy advocacy organization that champions marriage and family as the foundation of civilization, the seedbed of virtue, and the wellspring of society.

Human embryos are human beings. Thus, embryonic stem cell research (called therapeutic cloning), which involves "harvesting" stem cells and killing the embryo, destroys human life. This research thus violates a principle of the Nuremburg Code—that there should be no experimentation on a human subject when death or disabling injury will result. The term "therapeutic cloning" was created to confuse the public and present the technology as something beneficial, when in reality, it actually kills people. The same obfuscation was used by the Nazis to justify their experiments, which, though ostensibly designed to protect people, destroyed the human test subject.

On February 13, 2002, President George W. Bush's Council on Bioethics (which was established to advise the president on bioethical issues that may emerge as a consequence of advances in biomedical science and technology) held its second round of meetings. The topic was cloning. The principal witness was Irving L. Weissman, MD. Professor Weissman teaches biology at Stanford University and is a prominent researcher (using adult stem cells). He is also the main author of a recent report published by the National Academy of Sciences on human cloning. The report came to two conclusions: Firstly, "Human reproductive cloning should not now be practiced. It is dangerous, and likely to fail." Weissman himself refers to bringing a cloned human being through the embryonic and fetal stages to live birth as "reproductive cloning." For our present purpose I will refer to this as "live-birth cloning." Secondly, "The scientific and medical considerations that justify a ban on human reproductive cloning at this time are not applicable to nuclear transplantation to produce stem cells [often called therapeutic cloning]." I will refer to this form of cloning as "experimental cloning." Here a human embryo is created from whom stem cells are "harvested," resulting in the death of the embryo.

Nazi research vs. experimental cloning

During questioning by members of the Council, Professor Weissman stated that he opposed "live-birth" cloning because to support such cloning would violate the Nuremberg Code. The Nuremberg Code is, of course, a body of ethical norms enunciated by the Nuremberg Tribunal which, following World War Two, had the responsibility of judging the actions of the Nazis and their allies. The point of the Code was to restate and apply the established ethical norms of the civilized world. It is universally accepted today.

> *Regardless of the good that might be produced by such experiments, the experiments are of their very nature an immoral use of human beings, and justify the opprobrium of the civilized world.*

As we know, the Nazis killed from six to nine million people, most of them Jews, in extermination or "death" camps. Nazi laws had "defined" Jews and other "undesirables" as nonpersons. Eventually, these undesirables were sent to the camps for extermination. However, before the killing in the camps began, the Nazis had engaged in an extensive campaign of euthanasia against the mentally and physically handicapped, which not only foreshadowed but also prepared the way for the extermination camps. Robert Jay Lifton, in his book, the *Nazi*

Doctors draws our attention to a book written during the campaign entitled, *The Permission to Destroy Life Unworthy of Life:*

> [It was] published in 1920 and written jointly by two . . . German professors: the jurist Karl Binding . . . and Alfred Hoche, professor of psychiatry at the University of Freiburg. Carefully argued in the numbered-paragraph form of the traditional philosophical treatise, the book included as 'unworthy life' not only the incurably ill but large segments of the mentally ill, the feebleminded, and retarded and deformed children. . . . [T]he authors professionalized and medicalized the entire concept; destroying life unworthy of life is 'purely a healing treatment' and a 'healing' work.

Nazi officials announced that "under the direction of specialists," "all therapeutic possibilities will be administered according to the latest scientific knowledge." The result of this therapeutic treatment of "inferior" lives was that, "Eventually a network of some thirty killing areas within existing institutions was set up throughout Germany and in Austria and Poland." Essentially the Nazis were determined to "cleanse" the genetic pool simply to produce "better" Aryans. In their book, *The Nazi Doctors and The Nuremburg Code*, George J. Annas and A. Grodin reveal that:

> At the same time that forced sterilization and abortion were instituted for individuals of 'inferior' genetic stock, sterilization and abortion for healthy German women were declared illegal and punishable (in some cases by death) as a 'crime against the German body.' As one might imagine, Jews and others deemed racially suspect were exempted from these restrictions. On November 10, 1938 a Luneberg court legalized abortion for Jews. A decree of June 23, 1943 allowed for abortions for Polish workers, but only if they were not judged 'racially valuable.'

Later, the Nazis created the extermination camps for the Jews and other "inferior" races. In the camps, Nazi doctors engaged in inexplicably cruel experiments on the Jews, gypsies, Poles, and others. They exposed them to extreme cold to determine the temperature at which death would occur. They injected them with poisons to see how quickly certain elements (lethal to the subject) moved through the circulatory system. They subjected twins to all manner of disabling and brutal experiments to determine how genetically identical persons reacted to different conditions.

Were these experiments "inexplicable"? After all, some of the experiments were designed to preserve life—albeit, not of the subject, but of, for example, pilots who were forced to parachute into freezing ocean waters. The purpose of such experiments, in other words, was to yield a human good. The end justified the means.

> *It does not take an advanced scientific degree to know when human life begins.*

Professor Weissman undoubtedly does not believe his views have anything in common with those of the Nazis. Indeed, he would doubtlessly be offended at the suggestion that they might. But do they?

If human embryos are human beings, then human embryonic stem cell research (during which the stems cells of embryos are "harvested" and the embryos are killed) violates one of the cardinal principles of the Nuremberg Code—there is to be no experimentation on a human subject when it is known a priori that death or disabling injury will result. Likewise, experimental cloning, which creates embryonic human beings but destroys them in the process of removing their stem cells, violates the Nuremburg Code. Regardless of the good that might be produced by such experiments, the experiments are of their very nature an immoral use of human beings, and justify the opprobrium of the civilized world. We should not use the results of such experiments anymore than we would use the results of the Nazi experiments on the Jews, gypsies, and others. To hold otherwise is, effectively, to repudiate the Nuremberg Code, the very standard upon which Professor Weissman and the National Academy of Sciences rely to reject live-birth cloning (which they judge to be too dangerous for the cloned subject).

The only way that Professor Weissman can attempt to distinguish the two cases—Nazi research and experimental cloning—is to maintain that experimental cloning does not destroy human beings. Is that persuasive?

The debate over the status of the human embryo

Not at all. It does not take an advanced scientific degree to know when human life begins. It begins in one of two ways— either, in the normal way, sexually, that is, when a female ooctye, or egg, is fertilized by a male sperm cell; or, as with cloning, asexually, that is, when the nucleus of an oocyte is removed and is replaced with a nucleus from another cell, after which an electrical stimulus is applied. In either case, from that moment forward, there is a new human organism. It is genetically complete. From the first moment, the new single-cell organism directs its own integral functioning and development. It will proceed through every stage of human development until one day, it looks like we do. It will grow and develop, and it will change. But it will undergo no change in its nature. In other words, there is no chance it will grow up to become a cow or a fish. It is a living human being—its nature is determined—from the first moment of its existence. As the renowned ethicist Paul Ramsey observed, "The embryo's subsequent development may be described as a process of becoming what he already is from the moment of conception."

> *'Therapeutic cloning' . . . is the very opposite of 'therapeutic.'*

This is the fundamental scientific truth upon which all our moral analysis must be built. If we obscure this fact, it is impossible to think clearly about these issues. Sadly, many proponents of cloning and stem cell research are engaged in an enterprise to do just that—to obscure the fact that the human being begins as a single cell zygote, grows through the embryonic stage, through the fetal stage, is born and grows through the infant stage, through childhood, and through adulthood, until death. It was the same being at every stage, though it *looks* different at each stage. Professor Weissman admitted as much when testifying before the President's Council on Bioethics. Councilmember Robert P. George asked: "Would it be fair to say that before [the adult stage and before the adolescent stage and before the fetal stage] Dr. Kass was in the blastocyst stage?" To which Dr. Weissman replied: "For sure." Think of your own "baby pictures"—you don't look like that today. But you are still the same person. As Dr. John Harvey from the Georgetown Medical School's Center for Clinical Bioethics observed, "a human being is unchangeable and complete only at the moment of death"!

Nevertheless, Weissman and others pretend that the embryo prior to implantation in the mother's womb is somehow fundamentally different, different in its very nature, from the embryo after implantation. In doing so, they continue a long and unhappy chapter in which, I am sad to report, ethicists, scientists and medical doctors played a role. It started with abortion.

Development of the term "pre-embryo" to undermine human life

In 1970, *California Medicine*, the then-official journal of the California Medical Association, argued in an editorial titled, "A New Ethic for Medicine and Society," that in order to advance abortion, it was necessary to change traditional Western ethics. The article acknowledged this was a difficult task, and argued that "semantic gymnastics" were necessary—"The result [of separating the idea of abortion from the idea of killing] has been a curious avoidance of the scientific fact, which everyone really knows, that human life begins at conception and is continuous whether intro- or extra-uterine until death." In other words, the principal strategy to advance abortion was, from the beginning, to deny the basic scientific facts about when life begins.

> *Since the public did not like 'cloning,' cloning proponents decided, with breathtaking audacity, simply to call it something else.*

This same strategy has long been evident in the debate over the status of the human embryo. A few decades ago, the idea of the "pre-embryo" was advanced. This is a very odd term, since an embryo is an embryo from the first day of its single-cell existence. Of course, before implantation, one might say the embryo was "pre-implantation". But, does implantation in the womb, which provides the tiny embryo with a safe home and nutrition, effect a change in the nature of the thing that implants? Experts in embryology are agreed that it does not. For instance, renowned authority on embryology, Ronan O'Rahilly notes, "The term 'pre-embryo' is not used . . . for . . . it may convey the erroneous idea that a new human organism is formed at only some considerable time after fertilization." So why was the term "pre-embryo" used (one might say, "invented")? O'Rahilly provides the answer, "[The term] was introduced in 1986 largely for public policy reasons."

Biologist Lee Silver of Princeton University notes:

> The term pre-embryo has been embraced wholeheartedly by IVF [in vitro fertilization] practitioners for reasons that are political, not scientific. The new term is used to provide the illusion that there is something profoundly different between a six-day embryo and a 16 day-old embryo. The term is useful in the political arena—where decisions are made about whether to allow early embryo experimentation—as well as in the confines of a doctor's office where it can be used to ally moral concerns that might be expressed by IVF patients.

Thus, we can see in the history of the term "pre-embryo" that it was developed and used largely, if not exclusively, to mislead; to hide scientific facts about the beginning, and unity, of human life; to bolster support for a new reproductive technology; and to gain funding for experiments on human embryos.

Though the term "pre-embryo" is dead and gone, its "spirit", one might say, lives on. We find it today in the cloning debate, as we found it a few months ago in the debate over human embryonic stem cell research.

Semantic gymnastics aside, cloning is cloning

As the debate began over human embryonic stem cell research, proponents claimed they did not wish for human embryos to be created in order to be destroyed during experimental cloning (called, "special creation"). Rather, they wanted to extract stem cells from "excess embryos", those locked in freezers in IVF clinics with little likelihood of being implanted in a woman's womb. Today, those who wish to subject newly created cloned human embryos to destructive experimentation must confront their prior claim. If they meant what they said during the stem cell debate and did not wish to create embryos specially to destroy them, they can not support experimental cloning, for that is exactly what experimental cloning does.

What, then, did the cloning proponents do? First, they claimed a difference between "therapeutic cloning" and "reproductive cloning." As we saw above, however, all cloning—by producing a new human embryo—is reproductive. "Therapeutic cloning" is the very opposite of therapeutic. If it were "therapeutic", it would, by definition, have to be, in some way, beneficial, or potentially beneficial, to the subject of the experiment. However, since "therapeutic cloning" results—every time—in the death of the cloned human being who is the subject of the experiment, it is the very opposite of "therapeutic". It is, indeed, non-therapeutic.

> *The semantic gymnastics of the cloning proponents is not a new tactic.*

Cloning proponents, who had hoped that the use of the adjective "therapeutic" would confuse the public, were disappointed when public opinion polling demonstrated that the public rejected cloning, for whatever reason and despite the adjectival modifier. So, what did they do? They shifted tactics. Since the public did not like "cloning," cloning proponents decided, with breathtaking audacity, simply to call it something else. At first, they re-named it "somatic cell nuclear transfer," hoping no one would notice that "somatic cell nuclear transfer" was the very definition of cloning. Of course, it was noticed; so they shifted again. Now they call cloning "nuclear transplantation to produce stem cells." Notice how dishonest this is. Cloning involves a process by which the nucleus of an egg cell is removed and a nucleus from another cell in the human body (a somatic cell) is transferred into the egg. Again, as with "somatic cell nuclear transfer," nuclear transplantation—i.e., the transfer of a nucleus from a somatic cell into the enucleated egg cell—is simply another name for cloning. To pretend that the term "nuclear transplantation" involves something different from cloning—when the process results, and is intended to result, in a new, living human embryo who is the genetic dupli-

cate of another—is simply dishone:
nents added the modifier "for the pu
cells". But, as shown above, the *p*
process produces a cloned human emb
be "produced" by the subsequent and c
that embryo.

> **❝** I submit that this 'defense of th
> through misleading euphemism is pr
> cloning proponents are engaged in. **❞**

The semantic gymnastics of the cloning p
a new tactic. In another context, George Orwe
1984 and *Animal Farm*, spoke about this kind c
fuscation in his essay, "Politics and the English

> In our time, political speech and writ
> largely the defense of the indefensible. . . .
> ical language has to consist largely of euphe
> question-begging and sheer cloudy vaguenes
> fenseless villages are bombarded from the ai.
> inhabitants driven out into the countryside,
> cattle machine-gunned, the huts set on fire v
> incendiary bullets: this is called *pacification.* N
> lions of peasants are robbed of their farms a.
> sent trudging along the roads with no more tha
> they can carry: this is called *transfer of population c*
> *rectification of frontiers.* People imprisoned for year.
> without trial, or shot in the back of the neck or
> sent to die of scurvy in Arctic lumber camps: this
> is called *elimination of unreliable elements.* Such
> phraseology is needed if one wants to name things
> without calling up mental pictures of them.

I submit that this "defense of the indefensible" throu
misleading euphemism is precisely what cloning proponer.
are engaged in. Recall how the Nazis subverted the meaning c
the word "healing". Recall how they used the term "therapeu
tic" to describe not the helping of suffering people but the
killing of them. Can we be blind to the parallel use of "therapeutic" to describe the deliberate killing of embryonic human

s today? Does it matter that cloning is undertaken for a
ter good," to cure illnesses or infirmities? Recall that the
eliminated those "unworthy of life" in order to improve
enetic stock of Germany. Recall how the Nazis undertook
l experiments on concentration camp inmates in order, in
e cases, to find ways to preserve the lives of others. Never-
ess, would anyone deny that such actions were absolutely
thical? Suppose a cure for cancer had been discovered by
se lethal experiments in the death camps. Would anyone
ert that the experiments were therefore justified?

Is there any essential difference between these Nazi experi-
ents and "therapeutic" or experimental cloning? As we have
own, each case involves a living human being. Cloning pro-
onents might try to distinguish the two cases by saying that
e cloned human being has no "potential". But what "poten-
ial" had the inmates of the Nazi death camps, each already
marked for extermination? Did that make them less human?
Of course, almost miraculously, many of the inmates *did* sur-
vive the camps when the allies rescued them. Equally miraculously, frozen embryos, which some claim are destined to be
discarded, have been implanted in a woman's womb and
brought to live (and healthy) birth.

> *No one is safe from brutality so long as we think that it is only* inhuman *others who are capable of inhuman acts.*

Every embryo is, as we have shown, not merely "potentially" a life, but is a human being from the first moment of
existence. Furthermore, any living human embryo has the inherent "potential" to develop into a healthy baby. How disin-
genuous it is for some supporters of cloning to claim the cloned
human embryo is only "potential life" because they will man-
date by law that it be destroyed before it can come to birth. (For
that is what the Hatch-Specter bill S.2439 would do.) Regardless of its location, the human embryo, by its nature, is full of
potential, unless the actions of adult human beings deprive it
of the opportunity to realize that potential.

It is easy to think of the Nazis as evil, as demonic, as not
really human. It is easy to think of the Nazis as if they were

somehow different, different in their very essence, from us. But that is to miss the one essential point.

Alexander Solzenitsyn, a man who chronicled and suffered under another ideology that denied the dignity of each and every human being observed that "The line between good and evil is not between people. The line runs though every human heart, and it shifts back and forth." Communist Russia killed perhaps as many innocent people as did Nazi Germany. However, Solzenitsyn did not regard the perpetrators as inhuman monsters. Rather, he saw the essential truth—they were human beings, engaged in immoral acts. They engaged in those acts by de-humanizing the persons on whom their brutality was inflicted, and they did so in the name of (perhaps in the passionate belief in) a greater good. But Solzenitsyn reminds us that, unless we are willing to admit that for the best as well for the worst motives, we are also capable of inhuman acts, we will have no guard against committing them.

This is the lesson to be drawn from the gulags and the concentration camps. No one is safe from brutality so long as we think that it is only *inhuman others* who are capable of inhuman acts. Rather, we will be secure when we are willing to look honestly at the objective reality of our acts, while realizing that we, too, are capable of acts that violate the inherent dignity of another, and refuse to engage in such acts despite the good we believe would result from doing otherwise. In the debate over the cloning and destruction of embryonic human beings, this essential truth must be our guide.

6

Human Cloning Is Inevitable

Daniel J. Kevles

Daniel J. Kevles is a professor of history at Yale University and the author of In the Name of Eugenics.

Many people were disturbed by the news of the successful cloning of a sheep in 1997 and began to worry about the possibility of human cloning. The thought of human cloning has been condemned by religious, political, and scientific leaders as unsafe, unethical, or immoral. However, all new reproductive technologies were initially rejected before eventually becoming commonplace. In the 1970s in vitro fertilization was condemned by some of the same people who now condemn cloning, but now the procedure is common practice. Surrogate motherhood was also condemned before becoming widely accepted. Once human cloning becomes safe, it will be a common reproductive option.

On announcing [the] birth [of Dolly the sheep, the first mammal clone] in 1997, embryologists Ian Wilmut and Keith Campbell, who had engineered her, noted that she had been named in honor of the entertainer Dolly Parton. Wilmut explained, "No one could think of a more impressive set of mammary glands than Dolly Parton's." Parton responded, "I'm honored."

Dolly's birth was a milestone in the engineering of animals for food and medicine, but not everyone was as pleased as Parton by the event, much less by the implication that the same methods might be used to clone human beings. On the con-

Daniel J. Kevles, "Cloning Can't Be Stopped," *Technology Review*, June 2002. Copyright © 2002 by the Association of Alumni and Alumnae of MIT. Reprinted by permission of the publisher.

trary: since Dolly's arrival, the prospect of human reproductive cloning has been widely condemned by clerics and ethicists, politicians, pundits and scientists as unethical, unsafe and socially dangerous.

Yet human cloning will almost surely happen. In the past, other new reproductive technologies were also denounced at first; but then they were adapted to serve human procreational needs and ultimately became commonplace practices. Human cloning already has advocates—according to polls, six to seven percent of adult Americans, including, no doubt, many who cannot or prefer not to have children by conventional means. If human cloning is made reliably safe for both mother and child, market demand for it will gain considerable force, likely overpowering the residue of moral objection.

Moral opposition to cloning

At the moment, the moralists enjoy a strong advantage. Ian Wilmut himself opposes human cloning, calling it "offensive." Clerics of many different faiths attack it as a violation of God's order; ethicists denounce it as a denial of the cloned child's right to a unique genetic identity. Social critics warn that cloning would simply permit the rich to indulge in reproductive egomania or entrepreneurs to mass-produce superior athletes. In a recent report, a panel appointed by the National Academy of Sciences concluded, based on animal experiments conducted since 1997, that production of babies by cloning "is dangerous and likely to fail" and that human reproductive cloning should be legally prohibited. Laws banning it have been enacted in 24 countries, including France, Germany, the United Kingdom India, Japan, South Africa and Brazil. Calls for the prohibition of human cloning have been strongly endorsed by President George W. Bush and the U.S. House of Representatives, though not—as *Technology Review* goes to press—by the Senate [the Senate has not yet acted on the issue].

The outcry brings to mind the great biologist J.B.S. Haldane's *Daedalus*, a slim book of reproductive utopianism published in 1924. Haldane held that the Daedalus of Greek mythology was the first biological inventor (the first genetic engineer, we would say) because he was connected with the creation of the Minotaur through the coupling of Pasiphae and the Cretan bull. Daedalus escaped punishment from the gods for his hubris, Haldane noted, but he suffered "the age-long reprobation of a humanity to whom biological inventions are abhorrent."

While Daedalus did not offend the gods of his day, many people have indicted innovators in reproductive technology for affronting God, or ethics, in ours. Haldane's ideas were mocked in Aldous Huxley's *Brave New World*. In the 1930s, artificial insemination was promoted as a means to a radical eugenics by, among others, the American biologist Hermann J. Muller, a socialist and future Nobel laureate. At the time, eugenics had yet to be discredited by its association with the Nazis, and Muller, along with other biologists on the left, thought that a eugenic revolution could be achieved if outstanding men could spread their seed via artificial insemination. To Muller's mind, so "many women . . . would be eager and proud to bear and rear a child of Lenin or of Darwin . . . that restraint, rather than compulsion, would be called for." Muller was naive to think that women would eagerly make themselves into vessels for the sperm of great men, but his ideas were also thwarted by the moral conventions of the day, which held artificial insemination—even to compensate for a husband's sterility—to be tantamount to adultery.

In vitro fertilization and surrogate mothers

In the early 1970s, the British scientists Patrick Steptoe and Robert Edwards faced moral condemnation for their research into the creation of human embryos through in vitro fertilization. The medical ethicist Leon Kass, claiming that infertility was a social problem rather than a medical one, contended that such fertilization was not therapeutic because it did not cure women of that condition. Kass—now the head of President Bush's bioethics commission—insisted that by making embryos in the lab, biologists like Edwards were doing experiments on "potential human subjects" who might suffer birth defects because of the procedure but who could not give their consent. Paul Ramsey, a theologian at Princeton University, found implications of eugenics—now a dirty idea following the revelations of the Nazi death camps—in test-tube fertilization. He insisted that it was a manufacturing process that, if coupled to genetic engineering, might enable parents to choose "to have a girl rather than a boy, blond hair rather than brown, a genius rather than a lout." He wanted such fertilization prohibited on moral grounds, and so did the American Medical Association.

Haldane knew that although a given biological innovation

might initially be seen as a perversion, over time it could become accepted as "a ritual supported by unquestioned beliefs and prejudices." Acceptance depends on social circumstances and the purposes to which the innovation is adapted. The women's movement that began in the 1960s, by emphasizing a woman's right to control her own body, led a few women to avail themselves of the Repository for Germinal Choice, the so-called Nobel Prize sperm bank, a venture in Escondido, CA, that Muller's ideas had inspired. But the women's movement helped infinitely more to divorce artificial insemination from both its eugenics connection and its adulterous connotation and associate it with the simple desire to have a child.

In England, Edwards—confident in his results from in vitro fertilization with lower animals—effectively rebutted the warnings of critics like Kass with the July 25, 1978, birth of Louise Brown, the world's first test-tube baby, perfectly formed and healthy, a joy to her hitherto infertile mother. By the mid-1990s, more than 150,000 babies fertilized in petri dishes had been born, and with in vitro fertilization clinics proliferating around the world, the number today could be higher than 500,000. Follow-up studies of test-tube babies have concluded that, while twice as many come into the world with handicaps such as low birth weight, nine out of ten of them are no more likely to suffer from disease or disability than conventionally conceived children.

> *In the past, other new reproductive technologies were also denounced at first; but then they were adapted to serve human procreational needs and ultimately became commonplace practices.*

Surrogate motherhood, in which one woman carries a fetus for another, was also condemned at first as immoral and exploitative but has since become commonplace. Thanks to advances in prenatal diagnosis, many women at risk for bearing children with genetic or chromosomal disorders resort to abortion if their fetuses have lost the roll of the genetic dice. It seems inevitable that human cloning, if made medically safe, will undergo similar taming and adaptation to human wants.

According to polls, a majority of the U.S. public already

supports so-called therapeutic human cloning—the creation of cloned embryos for research, particularly on stem cells—and so does the National Academy of Sciences. President Bush and his conservative allies, including Kass, object to research cloning, saying it creates life only to destroy it, but they appear to be fighting a rear-guard moral action. The mere prospect that human therapeutic cloning will pay medical dividends has so far sufficed to block the absolutists in the Senate who want to ban human cloning for any purpose. If work with embryonic stem cells begins to yield actual treatment for disease, therapeutic cloning will become even more common in the lab than artificial insemination and in vitro fertilization are in the clinic.

> *Therapeutic cloning today will hasten the arrival of reproductive cloning tomorrow.*

Therapeutic cloning today will hasten the arrival of reproductive cloning tomorrow. Even without it, cloning techniques and technology are advancing rapidly. Since Dolly, cattle and pigs have been cloned, and so have mice, goats, cats and rabbits, with techniques that are said to be promising for overcoming the practical difficulties in getting human clones to grow. Human cloning research will surely yield still further improvements in safety and reliability—and someday, somewhere, lead a biologist to implant a cloned, embryo in a willing woman's womb.

Reproductive cloning will happen

The demand for human reproductive cloning is already evident. Calls for permitting it have come from gay men, lesbians and infertile couples who wish to have genetically related children, and from people who want to clone lost children or other relatives. James Grifo, a fertility specialist at New York University Medical Center, has said of cloning opponents, "None of them have seen the misery my patients are living through." Still, human clones will not be what some people expect—replacement duplicates of their sources. They will, like everyone else, be born as babies. Each will be genetically the same as its clonal parent, a new kind of identical twin; but since each will be shaped by environmental influences different from those the parent encountered, each will develop uniquely.

Yet human clonal reproduction will open uncharted territory in familial dynamics, especially where children are raised by their clonal parents. No twin has ever been called into being and then reared by its identical sibling. How the child will turn out psychologically and emotionally is anybody's guess. But that uncertainty will not stop prospective clonal parents, just as similar unknowns about how children will turn out have of course not stopped conventional reproduction.

Once reproductive cloning is made physically safe for the fetus, its enthusiasts may find an ally in U.S. law. The U.S. Congress, of course, could decide to ban human cloning for any purpose, claiming the power to do so because it can regulate interstate commerce, and a cloning clinic would be open to women from anywhere in the country. But such a law could well run afoul of the U.S. Supreme Court's ruling in *Roe v. Wade*, which, by upholding the right of a woman to choose an abortion, arguably implies that the state cannot interfere with how she chooses to reproduce.

The first human clone will probably be born outside the United States—perhaps in China, where work on human cloning is reported to be proceeding. Wherever the child appears, its birth will undoubtedly electrify the world. Unlike Louise Brown, this baby will not fade immediately into the noise of daily life; people will want to know with much greater interest if it is healthy, and if it remains so. If it does, one imagines that other cloned children will follow and become commonplace—beneficiaries, like Louise Brown's successors, of a new commodity in the growing emporium of human reproduction.

7

Cloning Humans May Be Impossible

Philip Cohen

Philip Cohen is a regular contributor to NewScientist.com

It may be impossible to clone primates, including human beings. During the cloning procedure, primate eggs, unlike those of other animals, lose a key set of proteins. This loss of proteins causes genetic chaos, prohibiting the embryo from developing further.

A newly discovered quirk of primate cell biology suggests that monkeys—and humans—are impossible to clone from adult cells using current techniques. The finding directly contradicts claims made by Clonaid, a company started by a UFO cult, to have created several cloned babies.

"There's a molecular obstacle that stops the technology from working in primates," says Gerald Schatten, at the University of Pittsburgh School of Medicine in Pennsylvania. "Charlatans who claim they have cloned humans clearly don't understand the biology."

Unlike other species in which adult animals have been successfully cloned, Schatten's team found that the eggs of rhesus monkeys are robbed of a key set of proteins during the cloning procedure. The same appears to be true for human cells.

That loss causes genetic chaos in cloned monkey embryos, with chromosomes distributed almost at random. As a result, the embryos look fine at an early stage, but are completely incapable of further development.

"It's an interesting part of the puzzle of why primates have been so difficult to clone," says Robert Lanza of Advanced Cell Technology, a Massachusetts-based biotech company that has cloned very early stage human embryos for therapeutic research.

"Gallery of horrors"

Schatten's group want to clone monkeys to assist in the study of human diseases. The key technology is called somatic cell nuclear transfer (SCNT), where a cell from the adult animal to be cloned is fused with an egg stripped of its own nuclear DNA.

Other researchers had cloned sheep, cows, mice, goats, pigs, rabbits and a cat, so Schatten was confident monkeys could be cloned too. But despite producing perfect-looking monkey embryos using SCNT, none developed further.

> *Despite producing perfect-looking monkey embryos using [somatic cell nuclear transfer], none developed further.*

New Scientist reported concerns about cloned monkey embryos in December 2001, when one of Schatten's colleagues described them as a "gallery of horrors".

The new study of 716 rhesus monkey embryos revealed the same chromosomal chaos. Some of the embryos' cells contained double the normal number of chromosomes, others had odd combinations and some had none at all. And Schatten's team have now discovered why.

Lost direction

On a hunch they examined the cells' spindles, structures that guide chromosomes into daughter cells as the embryo divides. The researchers found that SCNT primate embryos lacked at least two proteins required for proper spindle function, leaving the chromosomes to distribute randomly throughout the embryo.

These proteins turn out to be tightly linked to the chromosomes in the monkey's eggs, which are removed in one of the first steps of the nuclear transfer process. Further, unpublished work by Schatten's group and others has shown the same is true for human cells.

In contrast, mice and cows have extra copies of these proteins floating around to help out the cloned embryo. Schatten jokes: "It's almost like God in her wisdom said go ahead and clone cows and sheep, but if you clone a human I'm going to paralyse the egg."

Embryonic cells

The discovery is important, says Lanza, but there may be other important factors. Although attempts to clone a monkey by SCNT using adult cells have all failed, two animals were cloned in 1997 by embryonic cell nuclear transfer, which Schatten reports also creates the damaging spindle defect.

Furthermore, even trivial differences, such as slight changes to reagents, can turn success into failure when cloning other species, says Lanza.

Schatten intends to test his spindle idea by using a different cloning technique. He will allow the egg's chromosomes to remain in the embryo until after the donor cell has been fused, so the spindle proteins can migrate to new locations. He already has preliminary evidence that proper spindles then form, suggesting primate cloning could perhaps be feasible.

But he warns against any attempt at human cloning, given the high rate of abortions, neonatal deaths and health problems in clones. "I hope this natural obstacle affords us time to make responsible and enforceable legislation to prevent anyone attempting human reproductive cloning," he says.

8

All Human Cloning Is Immoral and Should Be Banned

The Vatican

The Vatican is the pope's seat of authority and the administrative headquarters of the Roman Catholic Church.

All human cloning should be banned worldwide, regardless of what techniques are used or what aims are pursued. There are three primary uses for human cloning: making babies (reproductive cloning), producing stem cells (therapeutic cloning), or for basic research. All three are an affront to the dignity of human life. Women used in cloning procedures are deprived of their innate dignity, as are the person cloned and the clone itself. Moreover, cloning for research involves creating and then intentionally destroying a human life. Since the United Nations' Universal Declaration of Human Rights asserts the sanctity of all human life and the necessity to protect it from harm, human cloning also violates international law.

The Holy See firmly supports a worldwide and comprehensive ban on human cloning, no matter what techniques are used and what aims are pursued. Its position is based on (1) biological analysis of the cloning process and (2) anthropological, social, ethical and legal reflection on the negative implications that human cloning has on the life, the dignity, and the rights of the human being.

Based on the biological and anthropological status of the

The Vatican, "The Views of the Holy See on Human Cloning," www.lifeissues.net, February 2003.

human embryo and on the fundamental moral and civil rule that it is illicit to kill an innocent even to bring about a good for society, the Holy See regards the conceptual distinction between "reproductive" and "therapeutic" (or "experimental") human cloning as devoid of any ethical and legal ground.

The proposed ban on cloning is not intended to prohibit the use of cloning techniques to obtain a number of biological entities (molecules, cells, and tissues) other than human embryos, to generate plants, or to produce non-human embryos and non-chimaeric (human-animal) embryos.

The biological background of cloning

Within conceptual and experimental contexts, the term "cloning" has taken on different meanings that in turn presume different technical procedures as well as different aims. Cloning in itself refers to the production of a biological entity which is genetically identical or very similar to the one from which it originated. The term is used to indicate:

1. The production of a nucleic acid (DNA, RNA), a protein, or a cell line starting from a single or a few copies of each of these entities. As no individual life is concerned, there are no peculiar ethical and legal questions on these processes.

2. The generation, in an asexual artificial way, of one or more biological individuals belonging to sexually-reproducing species (plants, animals, and humans). As animals and humans are concerned, this can be done either by disaggregating or subdividing an embryo ("embryo splitting") in its early stages of development or through the transfer of a diploid nucleus of a cell from an embryo, a fetus or an adult individual to a denucleated oocyte. In the latter case, if successful, after activation the reconstructed oocyte will develop into an embryo that is capable of further development to term. Regardless of its destiny, a cloned embryo is a cloned individual of a given species at the beginning of its life.

The possible purposes of human cloning

Human cloning is the scientific technique by which a human being is generated. The early but unavoidable result of both embryo splitting and nuclear transfer cloning is the reproduction of a human being at its embryonic stage of development. Thus, human cloning and human embryo cloning coincide, and they are identical with one another. Currently, there are three purposes for which human cloning can be attempted.

When a cloned human embryo is implanted in the uterus of the woman to which the generating egg belongs or of a surrogate mother, the delivery of a newborn baby is expected following pregnancy, as has been demonstrated by mammalian cloning. This use of human cloning has been improperly called "reproductive cloning" since its ultimate goal is to reproduce an adult human being.

> *Cloning objectifies human sexuality and commodifies the bodies of women.*

A second objective of human cloning is to generate embryonic stem cells for tissue engineering and transplantation or use in cell therapy. Once the human embryo is cloned, its further development is arrested before implantation (usually at the blastocyst stage) thereby destroying the further development of the embryo. The proposed name of this sort of human cloning, i.e. "therapeutic cloning", is misleading in that it confounds the purpose of the action with the very nature of the process at stake. Indeed, to produce embryonic stem cells a living human embryo has been deliberately created and destroyed.

The transfer of a nucleus from a human tissue cell to an enucleated human oocyte and the study of the embryonic development that follows may be performed with an aim to understand the genetic and epigenetic mechanisms of cell growth, potency, differentiation, regeneration and senescence. This kind of experimental design in cell biology has been called "nucleus reprogramming". Despite the innocent name, it involves cloning a human embryo for the sole purpose of experimentation.

Human cloning is contrary to the dignity of human beings

Even if cloning is pursued with the aim of making a human baby that will mature into adulthood so that there is no destruction of the human embryo, this activity is still an affront to the dignity of the human person. As a form of unnatural asexual reproduction, it represents a radical manipulation of the constitutive relationship and complementarity that are at the origin of human procreation as a biological act and an exercise of human love. Cloning objectifies human sexuality and commodifies the bodies of women. Moreover, women are deprived of their innate dignity by becoming suppliers of eggs and wombs. The dignity of the person cloned is similarly threatened because other persons and technological powers exercise undisputed dominion over the duration of this person's life or his or her unique identity. Reproductive cloning threatens biological individuality and imposes the genetic makeup of an already-existing person on the cloned person. In turn, the cloned person is commandeered by another's external and internal profile thereby constituting a violent attack on the clone's personal integrity.

> *Cloning a human embryo . . . would institutionalize the deliberate, systemic destruction of nascent human life.*

Cloning accomplished for biomedical research ("nucleus reprogramming") or producing stem cells ("therapeutic cloning") contributes to assaults against the dignity and integrity of the human person just addressed in the context of reproductive cloning. Cloning a human embryo, while intentionally planning its demise, would institutionalize the deliberate, systemic destruction of nascent human life in the name of unknown "good" of potential therapy or scientific discovery. This prospect is repugnant to most people including those who tightly advocate for advancement in science and medicine. Indeed, nucleus transfer cloning is by no means the only or superior way to tissue transplantation and cell therapy. The use of multipotent autologous stem cells of post-natal origin together with transdifferentiation approaches to tissue regeneration is a very promising alternative to prevent immune rejection in patients who have received transplants. In addition, the use of "wild-type" and transgenic animals is another way to disclose cell biology's genetic and epigenetic mechanisms. Medical experimentation on human subjects, as pointed out below, is a crime under international law. This prospect is morally and ethically repugnant even to those who generally favor scientific research. There currently exist alternative methods of scientific cell research that accomplish the same potential objectives without the need to clone a human embryo that will inevitably be faced with destruction. To create life with the planned intention of destroying it violates the basic norms of moral, ethical, and legal considerations designed to protect the individuality and integrity of each human being.

> *Human cloning should be prohibited in all cases regardless of the aims that are pursued.*

Since the founding of the United Nations, the centrality of the welfare and protection of all human beings to the work of this organization is beyond question. The safekeeping of present and succeeding generations of human beings and the advancement of fundamental human rights is critical to the work of the UN. The Universal Declaration of Human Rights reiterates the sanctity of all human life and the compelling need to protect it from harm. In this regard, Article 3 of the Declaration asserts that everyone has the right to life. With life comes hope in the future—a hope that the Universal Declaration protects by acknowledging that all human beings are equal in dignity and rights. With the right to life comes liberty and security of the person. To ensure this, the Universal Declaration confirms that each human being is an entity who is guaranteed a future filled with the hope of self-determination. To further this end, conditions that degrade any human being with servile status and deny the fundamental rights to life and self-determination are reprehensible.

To better understand these points, it would be prudent to take stock of our human nature at this stage. Each of us, regardless of nationality, gender, race, ethnicity, or religion, share the same origin and are destined to develop as members of communities beginning with the family, the natural and fundamental unit of society. We strive to further our goals for self, family, and country, but we also, as fellow human beings, are called to further the common good for the present and future generations across the globe. We do this to protect all who share and participate in the human condition. However, if some human beings are destined to serve interests that do not take account of these fundamental principles of human nature that are at the center of the UN's concern, they are reduced to a servile status that denies them the fundamental claim to life and self-determination guaranteed to all. To clone a human being—regardless of the goal—is to deny this person's basic ontological claim that unites him or her to the rest of the human family. This human being has no hope in a self-determining future because his or her individuality will be destroyed to further some research purpose or to enhance the narcissism of a person who has already existed. In either case, the cloned human being is reduced to enslavement that contravenes the fundamental nature of human existence—to be free and to live as a unique individual capable of contributing to the development of the self and society.

Human cloning contravenes basic precepts of international law

Various international instruments acknowledge that the dignity of the human person is at the center of international law. Regardless of the objective for which it was done, human cloning conflicts with the international legal norms that protect human dignity. First of all, international law guarantees the right to life to all, not just some, human beings. Facilitating the formation of human beings who are destined for destruction, the intentional destruction of cloned human beings once the particular research goal is reached, consigning any human being to an existence of either involuntary servitude or slavery, and being submitted to involuntary medical and biological experimentation on human beings are morally wrong and inadmissible. Human cloning also poses great threats to the rule of law by enabling those responsible for cloning to select and propagate certain human characteristics based on gender, race, etc. and eliminate others. This would be akin to the practice of eugenics leading to the institution of a "super race" and the inevitable discrimination against those born through the natural process. Human cloning also denies those subjects who come into being for research purposes international rights to due process and equal protection of the law. In addition, it must be remembered that state practice and the development of regional treaties have acknowledged that human cloning conducted for any end is contrary to the rule of law.

Human cloning should be banned

Every process involving human cloning is in itself a reproductive process in that it generates a human being at the very beginning of his or her development, i.e., a human embryo. The Holy See regards the distinction between "reproductive" and "therapeutic" (or "experimental") cloning as unacceptable by principle since it is devoid of any ethical and legal ground. This false distinction masks the reality of the creation of a human being for the purpose of destroying him or her to produce embryonic stem cell lines or to conduct other experimentation. Therefore, human cloning should be prohibited in all cases regardless of the aims that are pursued. The Holy See supports research on stem cells of post-natal origin since this approach is a sound, promising, and ethical way to achieve tissue transplantation and cell therapy.

9

Human Cloning Represents a Lack of Respect for Nature

Brent Blackwelder

Dr. Brent Blackwelder is president of Friends of the Earth, the U.S. voice of the world's largest network of environmental groups.

The rapid pace of scientific advances in cloning technology has outpaced public discussion about societal controls and the environmental impact of cloning. The earth is on the verge of experiencing a new kind of pollution—biological pollution. Cloning animals or people disrespects the species as well as the individual. Some scientists talk openly about redesigning, or improving, human beings and animals. However, before imposing such risks on individuals or society, scientists must have a solid grasp of what they propose. The history of the introduction of alien species into native ecosystems as well as the use of toxic chemicals in the environment are examples of premature actions that have caused significant damage. Human cloning should not be legal.

Editor's Note: The following viewpoint was originally given as testimony before the U.S. Senate Appropriations Committee on January 24, 2002.

Friends of the Earth is a national conservation organization dedicated to a cleaner, healthier planet for all life on earth. We are part of Friends of the Earth International which has

Brent Blackwelder, testimony before the U.S. Senate Appropriations Committee, Washington, DC, January 24, 2002.

member groups in 69 countries. I have been President of Friends of the Earth since 1994. My doctorate is in philosophy from the University of Maryland, with ethics being my field of specialization.

The Senate is now considering long-overdue legislation to ban human cloning. [The Senate has not yet acted on the issue.] The debate is being framed as one between modern medical science seeking new technologies for the prevention and treatment of disease and those who are trying to block medical progress. The purpose of the Friends of the Earth testimony is to present the environmental case against both human cloning and the closely related issue of human germline manipulation or inheritable genetic modifications ("designer babies").

At the outset I wish to note that Friends of the Earth acknowledges that many applications of human genetic science, including those using stem cells, hold great medical promise. However, the rapid pace of development of new technologies, the enormous stakes involved, the lack of societal controls to date, the failure to analyze environmental implications, and the fact that informed public debate has barely begun, all indicate the need for immediate legislative action to ban the creation of full-term human clones (reproductive cloning) and at least to place a moratorium on the creation of clonal human embryos for research purposes (therapeutic cloning).

Friends of the Earth is strongly opposed to S. 1758, introduced by Senators Dianne Feinstein and Edward Kennedy, and we offer a critique showing that not only does this bill fail to control human cloning, but also that it gives the green light to full-scale commodification of human life.

> *The real specter of a totally manufactured world is upon us.*

Environmental organizations are concerned with the accelerated pollution and destruction of wetlands, forests, mountains, agricultural lands, and wildlife which occurred during this past century. Today humanity stands on the brink of a totally new and alarming change in our earth, as well—a change which could carry us into an entirely new realm of artificial existence and a new type of pollution—biological pollution, more ominous possibly than chemical or nuclear pollution. Science now has the capability of creating cloned beings and designer babies and of crossing the species barriers which have for millennia separated plants from animals and some groups of animals from other animals. The real specter of a totally manufactured world is upon us.

The basic environmental case against cloning and engineering of the human germline manipulations (designer babies) is that these actions violate two cornerstone principles of the modern conservation movement: 1) respect for nature and 2) the precautionary principle.

Cloning and the principle of respect for nature

Environmental organizations embrace an ethic of respect for nature. Environmental organizations carry on a variety of educational activities to help people understand and appreciate the natural world. Some take people on nature outings, others operate or support nature centers. We strive to demonstrate the interdependence of humans and the natural world and the value of each species' contribution to an entire ecosystem. If a species is altered or wiped out, then changes to the whole ecosystem can be expected.

The very act of cloning animals or people crosses the threshold of respect for the individuality and remarkable features of each species as well as the individuals within species. The principle of respect for nature leads us oppose to the full-scale commodification of nature—whether it be humans, animals, plants, or landscapes.

The push to redesign human beings, animals and plants to meet the commercial goals of a limited number of individuals is fundamentally at odds with the principle of respect for nature. Even though many in the biotechnology business assert that their goal is only curing disease and saving lives, the fact remains that once these cloning and germline technologies are perfected, there are plenty who have publicly avowed to utilize them. Friends of the Earth has even been called upon to debate such people on national television.

Some proponents of human cloning and germline manipulations, for example, extol the virtues of "improving" on the humans, animals, and plants now in the world by re-engineering them. Here is what they are saying:

Lee Silver, molecular biologist at Princeton University, in

his book *Remaking Eden: How Cloning and Beyond Will Change the Human Family*, envisions a future in which the appearance, cognitive ability, sensory capacity, and life span of our children will become artifacts of genetic manipulation: "The GenRich—who account for 10 percent of the American population—all carry synthetic genes. All aspects of the economy, the media, the entertainment industry, and the knowledge industry are controlled by members of the GenRich class. Naturals work as low-paid service providers or as laborers. The GenRich class and the Natural class will become entirely separate species with no ability to cross-breed, and with as much romantic interest in each other as a current human would have for a chimpanzee."

> *The very act of cloning animals or people crosses the threshold of respect for the individuality and remarkable features of each species as well as the individuals within species.*

James Watson, Nobel laureate and co-discoverer of the structure of DNA: "if we could make better human beings by knowing how to add genes, why shouldn't we? What's wrong with it? Evolution can be just damn cruel, and to say that we've got a perfect genome and there's some sanctity to it? I'd just like to know where that idea comes from. It's utter silliness."

Lester Thurow, noted MIT economist: "biotechnology is inevitably leading to a world in which plants, animals and human beings are going to be partly man-made. Suppose parents could add 30 points to their children's IQ. Wouldn't you want to do it? And if you don't, your child will be the stupidest child in the neighborhood."

The proposed and ongoing genetic engineering today is radically different from the thousands of years of agriculture where crops and animals have been transformed through cross breeding of very similar species. Experiments in genetic engineering violate the natural species barrier. We have witnessed scientists inserting fish genes in tomatoes and strawberries, making goats which produce spider-like webs in their milk, and adding human genes to pigs.

The cloners like Watson and Silver want to engineer nature to suit their objectives and don't recognize any duties to animals and people who could be redesigned to match the scientists' own vision. There is no reverence or awe of nature but simply a desire to replace plants and animals with the scientists' selection of traits—all for the purpose of making money.

The Feinstein-Kennedy bill (S. 1758) facilitates the objectives of those just quoted because it would allow a completely unregulated commercial industry in human cloning to produce embryos that could be brought to term illegally under a reproductive ban.

To turn next to the practical experience with animal cloning, it is important to note that Ian Wilmot, the developer of the cloned sheep Dolly admits that almost all clones suffer serious abnormalities. The recent finding of premature arthritis in Dolly is one of the strongest indicators to date that there should be, at a minimum, a moratorium on human cloning and on commercial animal production through cloning. What parent wants to risk child that will be diseased, deformed or developmentally disabled after a few years? Who wants to eat food that may be harmful?

Recent polling shows that 90% of Americans do not want human cloning. One of the reasons is that no one should be the subject of an experiment without their consent. Any cloned child would be such an experiment. What Americans do want are therapeutic technologies that do not carry such risks. The *New Scientist* has just reported that a stem cell which can turn into every single tissue in the body has just been found in adults. The article goes on to say. "If so, there would be no need to resort to therapeutic cloning." Nor would you have to genetically engineer embryonic stem cells to create a clone. One cell fits all? . . . (January 23, 2002, "Ultimate stem cell discovered," *New Scientist*)

Cloning violates the precautionary principle

The precautionary principle is another pillar of the modern environmental movement. The basic idea of the precautionary principle is that before imposing significant risks on others or society as a whole, we should have a solid grasp of what is being proposed. The principle embodies the wisdom of ancient adages such as "look before you leap" and "an ounce of prevention is worth a pound of cure".

Thus the precautionary principle mandates that when there is a risk of significant health or environmental damage to others or to future generations, and when there is scientific uncertainty as to the nature of that damage or the likelihood of the risk, then decisions should be made so as to prevent such activities from being conducted unless and until scientific evidence shows that the damage will not occur.

A review of major environmental problems of the 20th century reveals a range of unanticipated and awful economic and environmental consequences as a result both of individual actions and various modern technologies. Had the precautionary principle been operative, many of these disastrous consequences might have been avoided. Here are a few examples in the areas of chemicals, civil works projects like dams, introduced exotic species, agriculture, disease and medicine where the precautionary principle was not applied.

The numerous cases of alien, foreign, exotic, or invasive species, which have beset North American ecosystems like a plague in the past hundred years, makes vividly clear the problem of unanticipated consequences. The federal government estimated that the annual economic costs of invasive species is over $100 billion. (US Office of Technology Assessment, 1993)

Some introductions of alien species have been deliberate. The starling was brought to America by a man who believed that our country should have all the birds mentioned by Shakespeare. Now starlings are one of the most dominant birds, crowding out native song birds. One of America's most important trees, both from a wildlife and a commercial standpoint, was the chestnut. Very swiftly a disease, introduced through a USDA [U.S. Department of Agriculture] program, wiped out all the great chestnut trees. No cure has to this date been found. Other invasives like gypsy moths, the Asian long-horned beetle, and Dutch elm disease still plague our forests.

> *What parent wants to risk a child that will be diseased, deformed, or developmentally disabled after a few years?*

The zebra mussel, which was probably carried in the ballast water of a Black Sea tanker, has proliferated throughout the Great Lakes region and now causes tens of millions of dollars of damage as it clogs up water pipes. A century ago the predatory eel called the lamprey got into the Great Lakes via the Erie and Welland Canals and devastated fisheries and persist to this very day.

The moral of this story is that the ecosystem disruption caused by invasive species not only devastates native flora and fauna but can be enormously costly. Another lesson is that biological pollution proliferates and reproduces and is not easily stopped if it can be stopped at all.

> **❝** *Many scientists and companies in biotechnology are prone to present only the best-case scenario.* **❞**

The precautionary principle was not applied when our society began using very dangerous chemicals in the aftermath of World War II. To this very day we have major and costly battles about cleaning up nuclear and toxic waste produced many years ago. A prime example recently in the news is the battle between EPA [Environmental Protection Agency] and General Electric over the chemical PCB [Polychlorinated Biphenyls] waste which still remains in the Hudson River decades after the PCBs were dumped by the company.

Other environmental disasters

Looking at civil works projects, our society did not think through the devastating effect of dams on Atlantic and Pacific salmon and on other fisheries until many decades after precipitous declines in fisheries had occurred. Now dramatic efforts are being made to try to restore some of the salmon runs.

In the area of genetically engineered food, Friends of the Earth exposed the presence in our food supply of genetically engineered Starlink corn, which had been approved for consumption only by animals, not humans. Starlink corn began showing up on grocery shelves all over the country. Despite being planted on only 0.5% of the corn field acreage, it contaminated 10% of the entire crop in the year 2000.

A decade ago in the case of mad cow disease, the public witnessed the vigorous denial by British officials of any connections between feeding regimes (cows being forced to eat cows) and the disease, and asserted that the disease could not jump from cows to humans. Now they have acknowledged their errors, but the disease has spread to Europe. In other medical news about recent knee surgeries where people have died, the January 20, 2002, *New York Times* headline reads: "Lack of Oversight in Tissue Donation Raising Concerns—Tight Rules on the Use of Organs Do Not Apply to Tissues". When the subject goes from tissue and organ donations to the deliberate insertion of inheritable traits, the precautionary principle reminds us that it is not just the patient but future generations who are going to be impacted. One cannot simply recall a bad judgment on inherited traits. That is the lesson of biological pollution presented above.

The great naturalist Aldo Leopold observed that the human role of conqueror is "eventually self-defeating because it is implicit in such a role that the conqueror knows, ex cathedra, just what makes the community clock tick, and just what and who is valuable, and what and who is worthless, in community life. It always turns out that he knows neither, and this is why his conquests eventually defeat themselves."

Many scientists and companies in biotechnology are prone to present only the best-case scenario. The Friends of the Earth recitation of fiascoes from the past 100 years of biological invasions as well as recent screw-ups in modern medicine show that our society must focus on more than simply best-case scenarios. The precautionary principle poses a direct challenge to uninhibited experimentation on people and the planet—experimentation done in the name of progress, but often driven by the desire to make money. The Feinstein-Kennedy bill does not embrace the precautionary principle but flaunts it.

10

Human Cloning Is Unnecessary

Thomas P. Dooley

Thomas P. Dooley is a scientist and CEO of two biomedical companies.

Proponents of therapeutic cloning promise that the technology will become a panacea for almost any illness. However, no type of research should be conducted when society has serious reservations about it, as is the case with human cloning. Proponents also fail to acknowledge that other effective, less-controversial treatments are being developed to treat serious illnesses. Therapeutic cloning involves the destruction of an embryo to treat another person, and the destruction of one person to benefit another is immoral.

In November 2001, a significant research event produced another ethical dilemma. A biomedical research company in Massachusetts announced that their scientists were successful at cloning for the first time a human being, albeit only to an early stage of embryonic development. It was a small step experimentally in producing a "new" human from the nucleus (containing the DNA blueprint of life) of an older adult cell injected into a manipulated human egg. The altered egg divided to produce a small group of embryonic cells. This type of method has already been used to clone other mammals, even to adulthood . . . so what's the big deal? At an experimental level, not a big deal, but at a moral level it was a HUGE deal.

As a biomedical research scientist and entrepreneur I've seen this train coming down the tracks for some time. I indicated in

Thomas P. Dooley, "No Imperative to Clone Human Beings," www.altruis.net, 2001. Copyright © 2001 by Altruis LLC. Reproduced by permission.

the media several years ago that our society was fast approaching new highly unethical practices, such as human cloning. Without compelling restraint scientists and physicians are moving forward rapidly to develop human cloning methodologies that could be used for either "reproductive" cloning to replicate another copy of a human or "therapeutic" cloning which would intentionally destroy the newly-created embryonic cells of the cloned human for other research projects. The same methods can be used for either desired outcome.

We don't currently have a signed bill from our U.S. government to restrict or prevent this practice, although Congressman Dave Weldon was successful at obtaining approval of a recent House of Representatives bill to ban human cloning for any reason. Our Senate is beginning to wrangle over this issue, and pro-cloning lobbyists are pushing hard to prevent a similar bill from passing the Senate. U.S. Senator Sam Brownback is leading the fight for a ban on human cloning. If this bill passed,[1] then President [George W.] Bush is considered to be willing to sign it. It is hard to regulate moral behavior using the law, but a signed ban on cloning would be a good first step. In August 2001, President Bush compromised on the former related issue in this debate and granted concessions to the proponents of embryonic stem cell research. Hopefully, he won't compromise again.[2]

Some folks just want to make copies of themselves or others. Perhaps even more people are touting the idea of "therapeutic" cloning as highly "promising" to provide a new means to treat a vast array of human diseases. The proponents confidently state this new science will become a "panacea-mycin". . . a single approach for almost any malady. Yet, there is no scientific proof of this assertion.

Let's consider some of the moral ramifications of this new cloning technology. It is important to note that any quality biomedical research, whether it is based on cloning or not, can probably produce some beneficial outcome. I'm a strong advocate for funding of biomedical research by our government in general. However, some research should not be conducted when credible moral objections can be raised. Spend the money on research that raises little or no objections from society.

Are we hearing from the advocates of "therapeutic" cloning

---

1. The bill has not passed.   2. President Bush has endorsed a bill banning all forms of human cloning.

that valid alternative research methods and therapies are already available to treat many of these serious human diseases? I don't know about you, but I'm not hearing it. In the haste to move forward the "whole" truth is being overlooked or suppressed. Outstanding advances are creating capabilities in research and medicine using pharmaceuticals, biotechnology products, surgical methods, and adult stem cells (not produced from embryonic cells). Human cloning is unnecessary. We can use other approaches to address research, treatments, and cures for these serious diseases.

Have you considered the profit motive? Please don't misunderstand me, I'm active in the biotech community and would love to see biotech companies grow and become profitable. The United States is the world's leader in biomedical research. Let's continue to produce returns on investments. That being said, some companies and academic researchers are moving forward with human cloning methods development because "there's gold in them thar hills". If the money trail dried up for human cloning research, then our well-trained scientists would simply work on something else. That's the nature of the scientific workforce. There is never a lack of scientific research questions to pursue, and employees will follow the trail to their next paycheck.

> *We can use other approaches to address research, treatments, and cures for these serious diseases.*

One of the central issues of this dilemma focuses upon the definition of a human being. Human beings are created with special attributes entitling them to treatment with dignity and rights. Yet, the advocates for human cloning view small human beings at early stages of life, to be mere commodities. Do we realize that human lives are being terminated in these experiments for the sake of the "potential" of a subsequent research experiment? Are early stage human embryos really human beings entitled to dignity and rights? The advocates of human cloning are saying loudly "no".

If they're presumed to be correct, then what's the difference between a one-week old human embryo or a 9-month old baby the day prior to birth or a 72-year old grandmother? When do dignity and rights begin, if not at the start of life? Is it morally acceptable to arbitrarily choose for instance that life commences "at first breath following birth"? I think not. Why is the life of the adult individual with a disease (desiring a new therapy) worth more than the intentionally-terminated innocent lives used in the research to attempt to provide a "promised" outcome from therapeutic cloning? Is human life that cheap?

> *Human beings are created with special attributes entitling them to treatment with dignity and rights.*

A related question is whether someone should ever profit from intentionally taking the life of another innocent human being? If a fertilized egg or early stage human embryo used in this research is a human life, then the intentional destruction of that life in order to obtain financial or other personal gain poses serious moral problems for the researchers, donors, and our society.

Furthermore, these medical and research procedures are not without genuine risks to the egg donors, the created embryos if terminated, the created embryos if permitted to develop into babies, and the surrogate mothers who would carry them *in utero*. It should be unacceptable to intentionally impose risks even at a minimum to the egg donors and the created embryos, just for the "potential" outcome from yet another experiment of dubious scientific merit. To compound this problem even further, prior experiments to produce viable adult mammals (e.g., sheep) required hundreds of manipulated embryos to produce one or a few "normal" adult animals. Most of the manipulated embryos failed to develop correctly.

We live in a brave new world, where brand new techniques are raising brand new ethical dilemmas. In politically-incorrect plain English, we are creating new ways to sin at a rapid pace. Yes, we can now sin in ways that were unthinkable a century ago, and only plausible 4 years ago.

Our Western societies are being deceived by many medical ethicists, researchers, physicians, politicians, journalists, and theologians who claim that if these researchers "don't do this critical work, then it is immoral", as if the cloning researchers are morally compelled to do this research for the benefit of mankind. Nothing could be further from the truth. There is no moral imperative to clone human beings for any reason. Many advocates are declaring by their own clever counter-intuitive rhetoric and actions that "evil is good", an inversion of conventional Judeo-Christian ethical principles. Oh! To the contrary, it is the very pro-cloning research teams and their associates that are doing the immoral acts.

This is a critical time to declare that research on human cloning is demoralizing and redefining human life. As a human being and coincidentally a biomedical research scientist, I find it simply detestable. I realize these words are not sugar-coated. I think it is time that we dialoged candidly and truthfully. We just don't need to clone humans for any reason. Give it up.

11

Human Cloning Will Redefine Families

Glenn McGee

Glenn McGee is an editor of the American Journal of Bioethics.

Human cloning is the reproductive technology least tied to intimacy. It is not generally associated with family but rather with egomaniacal villains in science fiction. Therefore, the impact of cloning on ideas of family and sexual life should be examined. Indeed, cloning will produce situations that challenge the traditional concepts of parenthood and family. For example, it is not always obvious who are the parents of a cloned embryo. Sex, reproduction, and family structure have been connected in a consistent manner for centuries, but human cloning will radically alter these connections. For instance, the mother of a clone could actually be considered the child's sister. In addition, the importance of sexual intimacy in procreation may become marginalized.

It goes without saying that human cloning does not involve, or need to involve, sexual intercourse. As one probes the seeming asexuality of cloning, one is initially drawn to the metaphors that feed and follow the asexual nature of the technology. Nuclear transfer of genetic information from a single human that results in the production, or at least is envisioned as having primacy in the creation, of another single human certainly seems to be the reproductive technology least tied to human intimacy. This is because it neither aims to approximate, nor synthesizes in scientific practice, the modes of pro-

Glenn McGee, "Cloning, Sex, and New Kinds of Families," *Journal of Sex Research*, August 2000. Copyright © 2000 by Society for the Scientific Study of Sexuality, Inc. Reproduced by permission.

creation that have historically been tied to the experiences, feelings, and needs of sexual reproduction. Images and ideas about cloning have been produced largely by the literature of science fiction and ring not with the love or longing of couples engaged in a sexual search loaded with procreative resonance, but rather with the self-love of particular and usually egomaniacal individuals. The bad guys on Star Trek make clones, or are clones, or seek the power of cloning.

> *It goes without saying that human cloning does not involve, or need to involve, sexual intercourse.*

But is cloning free of sexual charge, or merely charged in ways that clinical and social institutions have not yet developed a vocabulary to explain? Is the resonance of cloning in the literature of science fiction free of sexual charge, or is it in fact nuanced with all sorts of feelings of need that fall quite neatly into the range of human sexual expression? How would it feel to make a clone, and what sort of concern ought those who work on sexuality have about experiments with radically new attempts to envision the emotional meaning of procreative, or in this case recreative, activity? Perhaps the most interesting and important questions about cloning and the ethics of its potential practice, queries that been examined to death in the philosophical literature and burgeoning literature of bioethics, have been targeted at the wrong loci. Instead of a strict focus on the needs of cloned offspring or the limits of human procreative freedom, perhaps what is called for is proactive, prescient reflection about the ways in which the human cloning debate gets at ideas of family and sexual life that merit attention in the scholarly community of sex research. Not myself a sex researcher, but rather a scholar of bioethics, I come to that task with the goal of provoking such a conversation by recasting the problem of cloning in categories that are new to the literature on the ethics of reproductive technology, and by offering a brief review of ways in which cloning has been understood in my related area of research.

The human cloning debate presents an unusually complex and emotionally charged set of problems, several of which seem to be both new and unusual. A history of that debate is instructive. Preceded by years of comparatively quiet veterinary genetic research on nuclear transfer, the context of the creation of the first cloned mammal was about as unusual as one could imagine. Public discussion of cloning was promulgated by Dolly, a cloned Blackfin Scottish Ewe named for a country music singer, and inflamed by Richard Seed, a Chicago biophysicist (involved with embryo transfer experiments) who announced on National Public Radio that he planned to clone himself several times "for fun." Public debate about cloning, catalyzed by Seed, centered around the danger of a despot conducting cloning experiments that would in some way pose a hazard to the population at large, and on the dangers of homogeneity that might obtain from cloning pets and livestock. Virtually every philosopher with an interest in ethics was suddenly called on by television to answer questions, most frequently: "Is it ethical to clone a recently deceased child?" or, "Would a clone have a soul?" A LEXIS/NEXIS search of newspaper and major television and magazine stories in 1997 containing both the words clone and philosopher revealed more than 4,500 individual citations, 65% of which occur in March of that year. Within a year of the birth of Dolly the odd, marginal, and unlikely problem of human cloning had been elevated to one of the most hotly debated issues in 20th century science and health. Oddly missing from the debate were sexologists, scholars of the history of sexuality, or researchers in deviance and in family demography. The question "Will cloning take men out of the picture or eliminate sex?" was posed to bioethicists who lacked understanding of the set of problems, and was hardly taken up at all by the subsequent commissions and deliberative projects on cloning in the United States and Europe.

> ❝ The human cloning debate presents an unusually complex and emotionally charged set of problems, several of which seem to be both new and unusual. ❞

Philosophical debate about cloning has been mounted but along fairly predictable lines, with scant examination of the implications of cloning for human nature, social institutions, or the practice of basic biological science. The received ethical question remains narrow, focused on the limitations of personal procreative liberty (i.e., does anyone have the right to make a clone, and upon whose rights would such a process infringe. Two recent announcements have made this question seem urgent: the news that a clinic in Korea may have made a human embryo from cloned adult DNA, and reports of the need for creating human embryos from cloning in order to advance stem cell technology, including the fairly revolutionary project of Advanced Cell Technologies, who inserted human DNA into a cow egg to form human-like cloned embryos for stem cell research. However, the insistence of many thinkers that cloning be treated as a special instance of limitation on procreative rights has impoverished the broader debate about how sexuality and reproduction are changing at the turn of the century.

> *Genetic science of the 20th century impacts the way humans understand human capacity, meaning, and potential.*

Genetic science of the 20th century impacts the way humans understand human capacity, meaning, and potential. Genetics is intimately tied to procreation, sexuality, and reproduction, which are also the foci of the most intimate and invasive institutions, the family, medicine, and religion. When humans make children and when it is time to think of inheritance, one is building one's personal and communal understandings of loyalty, privacy, happiness, and growth. And, at the same time, human genetic information is rapidly becoming both a language of medical diagnosis and a commodity for licensure and ownership. Someone owns techniques for cloning mammals, including humans. It has become important to make social choices about the institutions that should be entrusted to reconstruct the family in an era of advancing reproduction, genetics, and cloning.

What is required is a focus on the biological, cultural, and common sense dimensions of human cloning. By selectively emphasizing and analyzing these three dimensions of the context of cloning, rather than rushing to more obviously normative aspects, one sees that human cloning is neither a special moral issue nor a radical step forward. Instead, human cloning is seen to be an element in a set of moral and scientific problems that compel scholars to reconstruct the enterprise of social thought about the embryo, the family and future generations.

Biological dimensions of human cloning

While there is an accepted biological definition of cellular cloning, and there are now well-understood (indeed, patented) practices for the transfer of nuclei from embryos or somatic cells into enucleated eggs, it is still not possible to define a cloned mammal organism. That this is so has not gone unnoticed in the biological and philosophical literature of the latter part of this century. Yet now that mammalian cloned organisms are among us, and human clones seem imminent, it becomes critical to ask anew how institutions and individuals are to obtain semantic and scientific clarity about the meaning of a mammalian clone? Must a clone have all of its DNA from a single other creature? Must the donor of a clone's DNA be an adult? Can a clone's egg come from a source other than the DNA source? If the source DNA contains a slight mutation, is the resultant organism still a clone? Must a clone act or sound or seem like its source organism, or perform that organism's role in the community or herd? These questions have not yet been answered, despite the use of clone as a descriptor for, at last count, more than 400 living mice, sheep, cows, and other mammals.

Received definitions of a human clone come from science fiction, not the lab. Stories of cloning have been used to illustrate the problems of nature versus nurture, the problem of defining the content of human character, and the problem of preserving our memories in future generations. Captain Kirk's transporter failed, splitting him into two Kirks, one aggressive and domineering, the other intellectual but indecisive. Fictional clones underwent "replicative fading" in *Brave New World* as they were copied one from another. Mostly, clones of our imagination have carried the memories, feelings, and ambitions of one generation into a next generation. Clones have been dupes and dopes, only occasionally rising above Dr. Frankenstein's monster's guttural longings. When it was announced that Dolly had been constructed with DNA taken from the udder of its progenitor, American fear of cloning was motivated and circumscribed by the clones of a hundred years of imagination. President [Bill] Clinton penned a letter within hours of the announcement calling his previously unfunded Presidential Bioethics Panel into action to prevent abominations of the family, with exactly these fears in mind.

What is a clone?

How one defines a clone seems to depend on to which side of the issue one stands. Those who see no problem with human cloning, such as Princeton geneticist Silver (1998) and Alabama philosopher Pence (1997), matter-of-factly compare any cloned human embryo to a monozygotic twin, which contains the same genetic information as its womb-mate sibling. Twins, it is noted, happen frequently in human life, and it is common today to keep one sibling embryo frozen in nitrogen long after the birth of a first. To avoid the pejorative overtone about clones and cloning, Pence suggests a new term: somatic cell nuclear transfer. By contrast, those who disapprove of human cloning technology point to the centrality of sexual recombination in mammal reproduction, and argue that it would be extremely difficult to predict either the viability or risks associated with gestating or being born a human clone.

> *How one defines a clone seems to depend on to which side of the issue one stands.*

Can there be a sober, agreeable definition of a clone? While the brute techniques required to produce a clone are getting better, embryologists cannot state with absolute certainty the genetic or phenotypic identity of a clone. It is impossible even to establish the genetic similarity of Dolly to its progenitor beyond checking a few patches of genetic code in a few cells. Dolly's status as a clone was confirmed in 1998 by analysis of restriction fragment length polymorphisms in Dolly and its dead progenitor ewe. However, the full sheep genome has not yet been sequenced and it is not yet possible to compare the complete genetic information in any two sheep cells. Moreover, Dolly is markedly morphologically different from its progenitor ewe, some 20% larger by Wilmut's own calculations. All this goes to the point that while it is possible to draw inference from our method and the morphological outcome of cloning, it is not possible to confirm what a clone "is" using scientific measurement. This is ironic given how easy it is to make a clone, and emblematic of the degree to which our ability to engineer outstrips our ability to measure the outcome.

A new kind of child

We think of the identity of mammals, including human beings, more and more in terms of the genetic code they bring into the world. A variety of new, urgent, and puzzling legal cases force adults to puzzle over the meaning of that code as it bears on parenthood and identity. When two mothers each give part of an egg, are both mothers? If surrogate mothers do not donate DNA, are they mothers? If a couple divorces, what role does each divorcee have in determining the use of frozen embryos they have previously made? If a man dies, can he be a posthumous father? These and more difficult cases have led jurists and legislators to create exceptional new laws about genetic relatedness. Biologists and the broader culture would thus like to be able to at least define cloning in terms of something stable: genetic similarity. Cloning, after all, seems to raise the possibility of a wholly new kind of child, one made not from sex or sexual recombination, but rather from the transfer of genetic information from a single progenitor into its offspring. But in reality, while one cannot know what sort of a human being a clone would be, neither is it possible to have any objective purchase on the variety of new kinds of children we make through new reproductive technologies and through new social mechanisms. Scientists may be able to determine the origins of a child's DNA, but that only begins the process of reinventing ideas of relatedness and how relatedness conveys status and responsibility. Clinical programs in reproductive technology have amazing new ways to make children, and society thinks of the reproductive technology process in increasingly design-oriented terms.

That this is so is a function of the biological, political, and economic history of pregnancy and childbearing, which others have discussed in much more detail than I will attempt here. Elsewhere I have drawn the conclusion that new genetic technologies and neonatal intensive care, as well as advancing diagnostic science, have changed the nature of the pregnancy experience from one of having to one of making babies. By this I mean that our best ethnographic studies suggest that parents of our time are able to identify with and care for a future child, and that their relationship to future children, including fetuses as well as those not yet conceived, is one that frequently feels like it includes an obligation to prevent future harm. Even sexuality is infused with this sense, as recent reports about fears of sex during pregnancy suggest.

> *// We think of the identity of mammals, including human beings, more and more in terms of the genetic code they bring into the world. //*

Despite a cultural insistence on the absolute right of a woman to terminate a pregnancy prior to the time a fetus is viable outside the womb, parents and social institutions are increasingly able to think of the fetus as a child for a variety of purposes. Thus, for example, parents who fail to care for their pregnancy, or physicians who fail to diagnose a fetal malady, are subject to sanctions or damages for the tort of harming a being that does not (at the time of pregnancy) have a right to exist per se, but seems to nonetheless have a right not to be brought into the world in a way that is harmful to it.

"Under the hood" of pregnancy

The identification of a parental responsibility to future offspring has been long in coming and is tied to a variety of changes in what individuals mean by childhood and what they expect of children and childbearing. In the course of creating the most recent birth and genetic technologies clinicians and parents have found a way "under the hood" of pregnancy, radically increasing the ability of adults to take care in choosing the time and manner of pregnancy. Parents use ultrasound, conduct amniocentesis, mix and match genetic parents, and screen for the most healthy embryos, all for this purpose.

For example, if a woman's eggs are in some way defective and if the couple can take a second mortgage or have a free credit card, they will be treated for infertility. Why? Because it is now said that wholly apart from the couple's need to make love to one another, they feel the separate need to have a biologically similar child; the need to do something to make such a child. The new tool of egg donation implies the possibility that they might ameliorate a new kind of need. They want a child; they want it to feel like their child, they want to give birth to it. The need to have a child of such specific parameters is a new kind of phenomenon, inspired by the culture's increasing tendency to think of fertility and parenthood as a state of affairs that includes both gestation and genetic relation. The couple's imagination is of a child that is "mostly" theirs. But a baby from egg donation, they are told, is not 100% their genetic child. They are not going to be able to completely emulate the "fertile" state. So, electing to use a donated egg, they are under the hood, tinkering with what for most parents is just a shiny surprise. Their child is going to require more planning. No more will sexual encounters be about making babies. Their baby will come from a dish. They control, or at least hope to control, what goes in the dish. Put more accurately, parents feel responsible for what goes in the dish. They won't want to choose a donor who has a dangerous congenital anomaly. If they can choose a donor who is more likely to produce offspring with traits resembling our own (height, eye color), they might spare their child the feeling of being obviously different from them. And if they are under the hood anyway, they might also make sure that one of their children is male, and pay a small amount more for a young, Ivy League donor.

> *In the case of a cloned embryo, it is not at all obvious who are the parents.*

That it is odd to be under the hood is obvious. That it is a different kind of parental decision-making, less subtle and more commodified, seems likely. But the point to be noted here is that advancing reproductive technologies exacerbate the evolving problem of assigning and enacting parental responsibility. Where the abortion debate focused the attention of the western world on the comparatively simple question of when an in vivo fetus takes on moral status, new reproductive technologies raise the problem of what it means to be a parent, and what value that experience has for those involved. In the case above, they will try to compensate for the 50% loss of parental DNA by making wise choices about the donor, choices that will both make them feel responsible and further assert a claim to dominion over the resultant child.

In the case of a cloned embryo, it is not at all obvious who are the parents. The person who donates DNA from a somatic cell is the progenitor, in that the child carries that person's DNA. But the mammalian parents of the cloned child are the grandparents, if what one means by parent is that the person contributed 50% of the genes to the recombination process that formed the genome of the person in question, rather than some idea about who most recently "used" the genes prior to their infusion into a new child. If the egg used to raise the clone comes from another person, as it would in the case of a clone of a male, there is in addition an egg parent, a person who contributes mitochondrial DNA and RNA in the egg wall, the collective role of which on an organism is unknown but perhaps significant. If the progenitor of the clone is itself an embryo or aborted fetus, the parent would not only be a virgin, but also a nonconsenting nonperson that itself has no legally established standing apart from the wishes of its own progenitor. Cloning makes acute what is already true in many new technologies and for embryology more generally in our time: Scientists and parents literally do not know what is in the petri dish, and make stipulative claims about our relationship to the thing in the dish based on a poorly thought-out set of ideas about intimacy and family.

> *By ignoring the importance of sex as a form and part of human flourishing, philosophers . . . miss the context of sex and its importance for the ethics of cloning.*

The empirically researched ties between institutions of family and practices of sex have often been misunderstood and misstated by the community whose primary focus has been ethics in medicine. In part this stems from what philosopher John Dewey called selected emphasis, namely the narrow focus on the rights and responsibilities of would-be parents engaged in activities that can result in the birth of a child. By ignoring the importance of sex as a form and part of human flourishing, philosophers . . . miss the context of sex and its importance for the ethics of cloning. In effect the debate proceeds along the puritanical lines of the ethics of parenthood and society, leaving sexual procreation as just another detachable experience to be conquered by technology.

> **"** While technologies for making children have changed quite a bit, most aim at and are measured against the story of the birds and the bees. **"**

Further, the complex and engineered nature of the cloning procedure makes each part of cloning difficult and interesting for those who would rely on any particular aspect of human biology for their ethical context. It is not obvious that a cloned embryo is an embryo. One part of what makes a mammalian embryo, after all, is conception. Sperm and egg fuse, and an embryo is formed. This is not so for a clone. An egg whose nucleus has been removed is fused with DNA from, for example, a human skin cell. The result is that the egg, in some cases, begins to behave much as an embryo. In the best of cases, that of the cloned mice from Hawaii, successful pregnancies of such embryo-like things result in only about 4% of all attempts. This is, or one might believe it to be, much less frequent than pregnancy rates for mice (or humans) attempting to have offspring through sex, though about the same as the rate of pregnancy from human sexual intercourse more generally. Put another way, a cloned mammalian embryo appears to be less viable than a noncloned embryo. What does it take to call the creature an embryo? Must there be fusion of egg and sperm? Must there be clinical potential, and if so, how much potential, that such a creature could flourish during gestation? Further, what is the bar for such a creature to count as a restoration of fertility, or as a therapy for infertility?

This last question is the most vexing part of the biological dimension of cloning. The felt need to parent is undeniable in society, and more than $2 billion is spent annually on the pursuit of biological parenthood through infertility medications and procedures. At one level, social institutions need to form claims about what sort of role individuals should be able to play in designing children: how far under the hood they should be allowed to go. There surely are some negative rights against governmental interference in procreative activity, and these perhaps include some right to experiment with technologies like cloning. But more problematic is what it means to provide care for those who have a need to parent. Elsewhere I have noted that it is a common mistake to assume that it is species-typical for human beings to have children that carry our own genes or are biologically similar to us. Thus, while it is fairly easy to establish that infertility includes an inability to contribute gametes or gestation to a child's birth, sequellae to some organic dysfunction, the rub is that one cannot always cure the organic dysfunction itself. The therapy for infertility is often a technology aimed at providing as many children as are desired by some parent or parents. But is infertility cured by providing this therapy? Would adoption cure the condition of infertility as well? Does cloning present a cure? It seems clear that the answer requires theorists of fertility and sex to rethink and reconstruct the way that the needs of biology as regards reproduction manifest themselves in individual and cultural habits.

Culture and cloning

I was raised in the 1970s with a story about what it meant to be a child. The idea was that parents loved each other, got married, made love, and babies resulted. Parents loved each other so much that they raised those children as their own, and made sure that they could handle the responsibilities of parenting, marriage, and career by organizing life in such a way that only one of the parents would work, while the other raised the children. It is the story of the birds and the bees. Birds and bees, of course, do not live that way. But the story has powerful resonance for many Americans, representing what has taken on the name "traditional family values" in political discourse, despite the fact that such families are increasingly rare. It is a story that links sex, reproduction, and family in strict terms. While technologies for making children have changed quite a bit, most aim at and are measured against the story of the birds and the bees. In divorce and adoption, for example, the model of the birds and the bees is used by jurists to measure degrees of variation from the norm, and to aim at giving every child some approximation of the norm.

The data are fairly clear that tomorrow's children will not be raised in the world of birds and bees. Perhaps the most apt zoological metaphor for parenthood in this time is that of the ants and the termites, who live in large groups with distributed parental roles. The 21st century American culture sees children most often raised by some combination of nongenetic parents, or by those who are not parents at all. More than 40% of those born after 1998, we now believe, will have more than one mother or father by age 18. The majority of American children are effectively raised in day care, while all three or four of their parents pursue careers. Many in society have held that a critical role one can play in the life of a child is that of godparent, coach, or foster parent, and many families in many ethnicities have well-articulated roles for these mentors. It is not accidental that for centuries many of these roles have been identified as parental in nature, despite the lack of genetic or biological connection of the adult to the child. Such is the case for ants and termites, who distribute the parental role seamlessly across many kinds of care-takers, most of whom have no literal gestational or fertilization link to the young. The model of the ants and the termites seems quite contrary to the sociobiological model of modern human reproduction proffered most prominently by Dawkins' Selfish Gene model in which all beings—and each being within the kind—seek to be parents by trying desperately to give genes to someone through sexual reproduction.

New stories

New technologies necessitate new stories. Octuplets and septu-plets will be the first in the human species to hear a story of the dogs and the cats; about being part of a litter. Humans need a story for a child whose entire first grade class, and soccer team, is comprised of siblings. Children of postmenopausal pregnancy will need a new story more fitting than that of the "accidental" late-born child of yesterday. Children of sperm and egg donors will need a story. While today most parents do not tell their children of the presence of donor DNA, eventually it will not be op-tional. Perhaps these children will be told a story about the race-horse bred from chosen samples of sperm, identified as a way of giving a child something in lieu of one's own gametes. Lions represent a story for children who are gestated by one woman, with an egg from another and DNA from a third. As transgenic egg donation from monkeys or cows finds its way into human reproduction, stories for that technology too will be needed.

But what story can one tell a clone? Already I have noted that human cloning is unprecedented in the natural history of mammals. Twins are the closest existing phenomenon, and unlike the clone they are born together and have sibling relationships. The stories of parental roles in cloning in the media are frightening in almost all cases. One has parents replicating a child who has died early due to an accident. Another has an infertile woman seeking a genetic link to her recently deceased husband through a clone from a tissue sample she happens to have lying around. Still a third has the parent raising a clone of his wife to realize his dream of seeing his wife as a child. It is difficult to imagine how a family would form stories for such a mode of intimacy, birth, and connectedness.

> *Humans need a story for a child whose entire first grade class, and soccer team, is comprised of siblings.*

The point of discussing children's stories is two fold. First, it is clear that whatever progress science makes in infertility, an important part of realizing the potential of such technology to satisfy the felt needs of adults is an account of what the technology will mean for the child. More, such family relationships are heavily textured by their social and institutional histories. Being tolerant of new kinds of families will have to begin with existing technologies and move out slowly and experimentally toward the margins.

But family is not the only sexual experience, and cloning would seem to have a significant impact on how sexual experience could be understood in relation to procreative activity. Following the host of other stories about how sex relates to family, cloning stories push the envelop in terms of marginalizing the importance of intimacies of various kinds in the personal sexual lives of those who want children and of those who do not. It could not be more clear that research must be conducted on the relative status of sexual intimacy in the minds of persons engaged in different kinds of procreative activity.

Second, children's stories—and the lack thereof—evidence the cultural manifestations of methods of satisfying parents' demands for children. The predominance of the story of the birds and the bees is symptomatic of a cultural and institutional commitment to genetic determinism, which in this case means a social faith that what matters about blood relation, and about relatedness itself, is programmed in and received through the genes of parents. People get married, make babies, and raise them in ways that seem normal because of their history, the habits passed down through the last three or four generations of western families. It is only recently that one could consider the possibility of lesbian or gay reproduction, or ponder the relative value of different kinds of offspring or relatedness. So efforts to squeeze every case into a standard of deviation from the normal model of birds and bees is merely a kind of collective dissonance with forming new habits about such an intimate matter. Families struggle with new technologies to restore the apparent equilibrium of the "classical" family, and work to find technologies that have as much explanatory power as the birds and the bees. This is one reason why, for example, most couples will use sperm injection rather than donor sperm. It is simply assumed that it is better and more normal to have a child that shares more identity with the parents. Thinking about and emphasizing the role of children's stories helps to bring these two issues into focus.

> *Habits in making families are only part of the culture of reproduction.*

Habits in making families are only part of the culture of reproduction. Parenthood is, at its edges, controlled and defined by the community and its institutions, and it is more than idle Platonic fantasy that children are in some sense raised by the state. I noted that economics, politics, and theology play roles in how infertility is understood and treated. The family is also only one among many institutions that raise children. In fact, when parents fail in a variety of tasks (from immunization to feeding to education), they can lose their parental rights, to be restored only at the discretion of representatives of democracy. The upstream manifestation of this public concern for the welfare of children is manifest when, for example, it is argued that future children ought not be exposed to the danger of cloning, or that research to clone humans is of a comparatively low priority in the existing array of choices for research spending. Even editors of scientific journals and newspapers have a choice about what they will send out for review and in what way they will publish findings about cloning. The culture has numerous options as its institutions are reconstructed by the rush to create and manage new technologies for parents and children. One is not limited by the concepts of family values or parenthood from the last 30 years, but neither can one invent ideas of familial rights without situating them in their cultural context.

Common sense and cloning

Cloning does not pose a unique challenge, but it has called attention to the vast array of new technologies that make new kinds of families whose parameters and relationships are neither pregiven nor socially sanctioned. It is insufficient to ask, as do most critics of cloning, whether a child of cloning would be deprived of a right to individuality. I have demonstrated that no child has an open future, and even our cursory examination of the changing history of parenthood makes clear that it is not individuality but rather responsible relationships and growth that are the goal of new procreative activity.

I have not addressed, in this essay, the tough or exceptional cases. Richard Seed wants to make clones. Greg Pence suggests the viability of cloning dead scientists. A Korean clinic may soon make the "first" clone. The tough cases are interesting, and many commentators focus exclusively and exhaustively on whether Seed should be stopped or Korea sanctioned. But the broader question is more important: What institutions and arenas are right for situating the debate about human cloning and its ken? Elsewhere Wilmut and I argue that the adoption procedure is a metaphor for what is possible: regional, localized evaluation of candidates for new procedures, accompanied by education and the social embrace of new families. But other and more experimental methods too may be called for. The claim of this essay is that the need to reconstruct the entire enterprise of making children in the 21st century is a necessary backdrop for debate about human cloning. Once this is accomplished, we can move beyond exceptional approaches to general problems and develop new institutional and personal habits for making and supporting families in the 21st century. More important, only then will it be possible to develop a systematic research agenda that brings the study of sex into the bioethical debate about what it means to be human in a time when reproduction and procreation requires so little ordinary physical intimacy.

12

The Human Cloning Debate Is Marred by Hyperbole and Science Fiction

Stephen S. Hall

Stephen S. Hall is the author of Merchants of Immortality, *an account of the scientific, social, and political roots of the current controversies over stem cells, cloning, and attempts to extend the human life span.*

Much of the interest in the subject of human cloning was generated after the announcement by a cult that it had produced the world's first cloned human. The press and politicians have overreacted to such sensational and often unsubstantiated claims ever since. Unfortunately, the hyperbole marring cloning debates has led to confusion and fear in the general public. This confusion and fear has led to a great rush to ban cloning even before the science has a chance to mature. We must bring more science and less emotion to the discussion of human cloning.

As any well-informed newspaper reader knows by now, the white-robed prophet Rael (nee Claude Vorilhon) is a soft-spoken, French-born, Canadian-based apostle of cloning technology who claims to have been conceived by a human mother and a space alien. The former race car driver also claims to have had two encounters with aliens in the 1970s and to have boarded their spaceship. He believes that humans were created

Stephen S. Hall, "Eve Redux: The Public Confusion over Cloning," *The Hastings Center Report*, May/June 2003. Copyright © 2003 by The Hastings Center. Reproduced by permission.

by cloning techniques developed by alien civilizations, and he has established a sect called the Raelians to promote human reproductive cloning, to the point of forming a private company called Clonaid. Rael considers himself a half-brother to Jesus Christ and requests that visitors address him as "Your Holiness."

> *The public, and policymakers, have been poorly served by the quality of this important bioethical discussion.*

In the calculus of most working journalists, the combination of UFO-ology, prophetic megalomania, and alien conception would ordinarily land Rael and his followers on the gentle, lowland slopes of any credibility curve. And yet a steady stream of writers—sometimes from prominent publications—have made the pilgrimage to "U.F.O.-land" in Valcourt, Quebec, to interview Rael (apparently some even agreed to submit questions in advance and call him "Your Holiness"). For its loony entertainment value, Rael and his be-robed colleagues make for an irresistible human interest story, but that also helps explain why Raelian claims to have created a cloned human child named "Eve" received such widespread and frenzied attention in the press in December 2002. Although the sect did not provide a shred of scientific evidence to back up its claim, the news prompted a familiar, even reflexive cultural reaction: social conservatives fulminated, the president reiterated his absolute opposition to all forms of cloning, and respectable scientists were left shaking their heads.

In a larger sense, that reaction helps explain why the national debate on cloning and stem cell research has so often spun off the road and into a ditch of techno-social voyeurism, ideological rhetoric, and political histrionics. While reporting for my book *Merchants of Immortality*, I've been a front-row observer to many events in this debate, and I've been struck by several recurrent themes: overreaction by both the press and politicians to sensational (and often unsubstantiated) claims, the absence of critical judgment in assessing these claims, the role of private entities (whether biotech companies or sects) in setting the tempo and terms of the public debate with their announcements, and a devaluation of science in the overall discourse. The public, and policymakers, have been poorly served by the quality of this important bioethical discussion.

A key moment in this debate occurred in August 2001, at a workshop on cloning sponsored by the National Academy of Sciences [NAS], because it revealed an illuminating gap between the rigorous, devil-in-the-details ethos of science and the rather more superficial world of public perception. Rudolf Jaenisch, a biologist at the Whitehead Institute, described detailed molecular studies that identified a series of glitches embedded in the DNA of cloned mice. These so-called "epigenetic" flaws—aberrations in the regulation or expression of genes but not in the genetic sequence of the genes themselves—could trigger arrested development or serious post-natal dysfunction. After Jaenisch laid out the data, a member of the National Academy panel directed a question at Brigitte Boisselier, the head scientist of Clonaid, who had previously described the Raelians' intent to clone human babies. What, she was asked, was Clonaid doing to identify the sort of epigenetic flaws that Jaenisch's group had described in the scientific literature?

Boisselier dipped her head politely, smiled reassuringly, and announced in an eerily lilting voice that Clonaid scientists had already developed molecular assays to test for ten such epigenetic flaws in human embryos. The claim was absurd. I was sitting in the audience that day, and almost fell out of my chair. Developing reliable molecular probes for such potential genetic aberrations would tax the ingenuity and resources of any top-flight laboratory, probably for years. Several members of the NAS panel of experts reacted with an unusually public display of scorn to Boisselier's claim, rolling their eyes or shaking their heads in disgust. "Ludicrous," grunted Alan Trounson, an Australian in vitro fertilization expert.

Yet the preposterousness of Boisselier's claim is, for most lay readers, probably lost in the fog of scientific minutiae, and that is the haze into which much of the substance of this debate has disappeared. I had expected Trounson's bluntly dismissive tone to permeate news accounts of the National Academy forum the following day, but I was surprised. While the accounts were skeptical, they were politely so, and more attention was focused on the intent of the would-be cloners than on a clear-eyed assessment of their chances of success. And so it hardly came as a surprise that when Brigitte Boisselier held a press conference on 27 December 2002, to announce the birth of the world's first human clone, the press greeted the news in similar fashion: it dutifully reported the claim, but it remained perhaps a little too polite and a little slow to contextualize and critically assess the scientific claims. The claim, however dubious, made front-page news around the world, and served as a global infomercial for Raelian philosophy. "Some media experts say we got between $600 million and $700 million worth of coverage," Rael later boasted, "and I did nothing." Neither, apparently, did the Raelian cloners. By January 2003, Rael was also conceding to some interviewers that he couldn't deny the baby clone was a hoax.

In one sense, the purported birth of "Eve," the first human clone, was an aberration; within days of the initial claim, the event had the odor of a hoax—as it should have had to anyone with passing familiarity with either the technical vicissitudes of cloning ("somatic cell nuclear transfer," to use the technical term) or the savvy self-marketing of the Raelians. But in another sense, the short, nasty, and brutal life of this unconfirmable story is emblematic of precisely the types of events that have convulsed the national debate about cloning and, earlier, embryonic stem cells over the past few years. Each such revelation triggers a drearily familiar set-piece: lawmakers threaten legislation, social conservatives express moral outrage, scientists run for cover, and the public is left feeling fearful and confused.

> *The claim, however dubious, made front-page news around the world, and served as a global infomercial for Raelian philosophy.*

The public debate on cloning, as on embryonic stem cells, has repeatedly been driven by these extra-scientific (not to say extraterrestial) announcements mediated by the press. These events undoubtedly qualify as news, and yet at the same time do not qualify as science—if we understand the latter to be a rigorously executed, socially responsible, and peer-reviewed published piece of experimentation that, pending reproducibility, at least has the whiff of truth about it. If the ethical implications of this research are too important to be left to scientists alone, as many observers have correctly asserted, it is also true that the scientific details of this research are too important to be misunderstood, misrepresented, or dismissed by non-scientists—that includes not only members of the media, but also politicians, ideologues, entrepreneurs, bioethicists, and even the scientists who sometimes imply too strenuously that therapeutic cloning and stem cell therapy will surely cure human disease. The first casualty in a heated political debate about science is complexity, and modern biological science is nothing if not a monument to complexity.

When I was a young aspiring writer living in Rome, I was asked by a prominent business newspaper to cover financial news, a topic about which I had no training and no knowledge. The request came on a Friday. Over the weekend, I purchased a copy of "Teach Yourself Economics." On Monday, I began filing dispatches.

I mention this because on any given story, especially on technical topics like stem cells and cloning, news coverage will reflect a broad spectrum of expertise and inexperience, and this becomes a factor in the public life of a technological idea. In point of fact, the Eve announcement received judicious and skeptical treatment in major newspapers, which reported the "news" (as indeed is their mission to do) but kept this dubious claim off the front page. Nonetheless, a certain politesse operates in objective journalism that renders critical assessment subservient to even-handedness. I would argue that critical judgment—not technical understanding, not explanatory skill, not even literary talent—is the single most important quality for anyone who aspires to write about science and technology; it is also, by far, the most difficult skill to acquire. The absence of critical judgment, the demands of competition, and the unremitting pressure of deadlines helps create the kind of media epiphenomena that characterized the cloning of Eve and the earlier announcement of the creation of cloned human embryos by the Massachusetts company Advanced Cell Technology.

Critical judgment becomes especially important in this arena because so much information is obscured by a proprietary fog; "news" is often released without prior peer-review publication, and always with an eye toward maximum publicity. Much of cloning and stem cell research is conducted by the private sector or with private funding, outside the purview of the NIH [National Institutes of Health]; there is no federal pressure or moral suasion to be candid with the public. Indeed, when bioethicists who advise private companies refuse to discuss ongoing research, as has happened in my experience, they promote (however reluctantly) the privatization of a national debate that requires absolute transparency.

In the last year or so, several bioethicists I respect have intimated that science writers too often function as mindless cheerleaders of technological innovation, that they are camp followers who plunge headlong in the direction of Progress while leaving their moral compasses at home. Speaking only for myself, I do not see my role as that of a cheerleader, but I plead guilty to a fascination with serious intellectual inquiry, aided by powerful technologies, to attain new knowledge, new understanding, and new plateaus of appreciation for the natural world in which we live. In fact, over the years I've managed to offend many of my secular humanist friends (my background is in English literature) by suggesting that science represents the last avant garde in contemporary society. By that I mean not only a loosely institutionalized quest for the new, but a kind of New that has the power to force society to rethink some of its most basic premises. Many of the bioethical debates we are now having attest to the power of the changes wrought, or promised, by contemporary biology, and in fact were anticipated many decades ago by the American philosopher John Dewey. In his 1922 book *Human Nature and Conduct*, John Dewey wrote, "situations into which change and the unexpected enter are a challenge to intelligence to create new principles. Morals must be a growing science if it is to be a science at all, not merely because all truth has not yet been appropriated by the mind of man, but because life is a moving affair in which old moral truth ceases to apply." To the extent that science, too, is a moving affair, it constantly challenges the traditional notion that moral wisdom is fixed and absolute.

> *The public debate on cloning, as on embryonic stem cells, has repeatedly been driven by these extra-scientific (not to say extraterrestrial) announcements mediated by the press.*

Setting aside for a moment the suspicion that so much indignant ink, legislative breast-beating, and ideological emotion about Eve may have been expended on a non-event, there were very good scientific reasons to suspect the Raelian claim was a hoax. Indeed, the scientific odds against a successful human clone—and by success, I mean the creation of a viable, genetically intact embryo that develops into a normal, healthy child—are overwhelming. The success rate in animal cloning experiments varies from species to species, but has always been very low, on the order of 3 or 4 per cent. In primates—the animals closest to humans on the phylogenetic ladder—hundreds of cloning experiments have failed to produce a single viable embryo, much less a live birth. Anyone who has sat through a recitation of this dismal data at a scientific meeting (and I have) becomes an instant agnostic about the prospects for a healthy human clone any time soon.

> *This shear between public and professional perception brings us closer to the underlying structural flaw of the entire debate.*

An equally distressing media circus occurred in November 2001, when researchers at ACT [Advanced Cell Technology], including Jose Cibelli, announced they had created "the first human cloned embryo." The disconnect between the scientific and cultural appraisal of this experiment underscores the problem of critical judgment. While Harold Varmus, former director of the NIH, and Harvard biologist Douglas Melton were writing that the experiment "showed little experimental progress and advanced no new ideas," the editor of *Scientific American*, which published an "exclusive" account of the work, was telling reporters the ACT research represented "one of the major landmarks of biotechnology achievement in the past decade."

This shear between public and professional perception brings us closer to the underlying structural flaw of the entire debate. The National Institutes of Health has been relegated, by politics and long-standing social divisions, to a diminished role in supporting, monitoring, and shaping stem cell and cloning research (a role to which it has been consigned in reproductive medicine for more than twenty-five years). As a result, this area of science and technology has been driven by private enterprise rather than public accountability, lurid rhetoric rather than the rigor of scientific fact.

The private sector development of in vitro fertilization in the United States grew directly out of the failure of the government to act in the 1970s on recommendations by a pioneering bioethics panel, the National Commission for the Protection of Human Subjects of Biomedical and Behavioral Research, which concluded that fetal and embryo research was a legitimate area of scientific inquiry worthy of federal funding but that such research required the consideration and approval of an Ethics Advisory Board. As many readers of the Hastings Center Report no doubt recall, the Ethics Advisory Board's recommendation to support research in reproductive medicine was never implemented, and that goes a long way toward explaining why we're having the same old disagreements today, focused though they are on a newer technology. Although the EAB considered, and ultimately approved, federal funds for in vitro fertilization research (including the study of embryos created by IVF that might ultimately be sacrificed), Patricia Harris, then secretary of HEW, refused to grant final approval, and then allowed the charter of the ethics board to expire—even though federal regulations required its approval for certain types of research to proceed. The practical effect of this limbo has been that reproductive medicine, including research on infertility and fertilization technology, was ceded to the private sector, and very few researchers in reproductive medicine sought funding from the NIH. That appears to be the evolving case with embryonic stem cells as well. A highly placed NIH official recently confided to me that the agency has been surprised that so few researchers have applied for stem cell funding.

> **❝** *Although the privatization of research has its roots in the 1970s, history has repeated itself more recently.* **❞**

Although the privatization of research has its roots in the 1970s, history has repeated itself more recently. Corporate funding for human embryonic stem cell research grew directly out of the Clinton administration's famous repudiation of the NIH's 1994 Human Embryo Research Panel report, which advocated federal funding for a broad spectrum of embryo research, including the creation of embryos for research purposes. The flight to private funding sources accelerated when Congress in 1996 passed a ban on federal funding for any form of embryo research—a ban enacted without public debate by conservative Republicans in the House of Representatives.

This decades-long ability of politics to trump expert scientific judgment has shaped the rhetorical environment in which our current discussions take place. Scientific fact and judgment have increasingly been estranged from the conversation. Much of the "debate" over embryonic stem cell research, for example, hinged on assertions that adult stem cell research promises the same clinical benefits without any of the same ethical vexations. Those assertions are at their core scientifically based, with profound medical implications for all Americans, and yet you would be hard-pressed to find more than a handful of scientists who subscribe to that argument.

> *This same devaluation of scientific knowledge has long been a feature of the cloning debate.*

One of those scientists, David Prentice of Indiana State University, advised senators, testified in Congress, and was quoted in countless media reports, yet he had not published a single peer-reviewed research article on stem cells and in fact had been turned down for an NIH grant for stem cell-related work. As Thomas Murray has suggested, the opponents of embryonic stem cell research may have learned a tactic from the tobacco industry: that of creating the appearance of a scientific controversy or disagreement when in reality there was none. In a 2001 report on stem cell research, the NIH reflected the judgment of the overwhelming majority of scientists in suggesting that it is too early in the scientific story to choose one technology over the other.

This same devaluation of scientific knowledge has long been a feature of the cloning debate. Reproductive cloning (to create children) is widely and legitimately opposed, not least because of safety issues, but it has become rhetorically coupled to therapeutic, or research, cloning (which seeks to create short-lived embryos from which embryonic stem cells can be harvested, for both research and perhaps therapeutic applications). Opponents of cloning argue that research cloning will inevitably lead to reproductive cloning, and that the instrumentalization of nascent human life is a moral line that should never be crossed. But these important moral concerns hinge on scientific distinctions that are either misunderstood or largely ignored.

Representative David Weldon, who has sponsored several bills in the House of Representatives to ban all forms of human cloning (including cloning for research), asserted during a House debate in July 2001, "The biological fact is, and I say this as a scientist and as a physician, that [cloned embryos] are indistinguishable from a human embryo that has been created by sexual fertilization." In terms of genetic integrity and life potential, at the very least, this is demonstrably incorrect. A "natural" embryo has, at best, a 28 per cent chance of resulting in a human life, and perhaps as little as 14 per cent—much less potential than many people are aware. But a cloned embryo has, according to current knowledge, even less potential. Part of the reason is that the vast majority of cloned embryos appear to be genetically flawed. Research by Rudolf Jaenisch's lab has documented that many genes in the cloned embryo are dysfunctional, probably due to incomplete reprogramming.

These scientific facts about the minimal "nascence" of nascent life should inform our thinking about the moral significance of embryos as they cross successive developmental thresholds, which in turn should inform discussions about the ethical acceptibility of this research. For the most part, they have not.

Ironically, the rise of in vitro fertilization has resulted in the creation of hundreds of thousands of human embryos that, if not strictly for research purposes, are destined to be discarded as a by-product of medical utility. By some estimates, American fertility clinics created as many as 600,000 embryos between 1991 and 2001, and most were destroyed—a price society appears willing to pay to treat infertility. It is hard to argue that creating cloned human embryos for research purposes, with their even more limited potential for life and their considerable potential to relieve human suffering, represents a significantly different moral threshold.

That moral paradox brings me to a final observation. I've been struck, and a little disappointed, by how much the current debate has been driven by the promise of medical utility rather than by the value of basic knowledge. Although the possible human medical benefits of embryonic stem cells and therapeutic cloning are not difficult to surmise, equal value lies in basic research on human development—a compelling biological mystery that has fascinated humanity's keenest minds since Aristotle. While some have made the argument that to instrumentalize this nascent human life is an affront to human dignity, I see it differently; to refrain from plumbing the mystery of human life, on the only planet known to possess any life at all, when we have the ethical infrastructure to do it both wisely and well, seems to mark a retreat from the way we have pursued knowledge for many centuries. When anatomists first began to conduct human dissections during the dawn of the Renaissance, it provoked great moral anguish and a sense of violation that, at some level, must have seemed like an affront to human dignity. But then as now, the preservation of an abstract notion of human dignity may have as a material cost the willful preservation of human ignorance and a perverse perpetuation of human suffering.

Until we bring more rigor and less emotion to our discussion of these new technologies, our public policy will again and again become hostage to hoaxes, publicity stunts, and rhetorical excess. Late in March 2003, Brigitte Boisselier and Rael were back in the news, popping up in Sao Paulo, Brazil, to announce that Clonaid had successfully created five human clones. As before, they did not produce any scientific evidence to support the claim, and as before, the press dutifully passed along the news. Why Sao Paulo? As the Reuters account noted, Boisselier and Rael "were in Brazil to present Rael's book on cloning."

Organizations to Contact

The editors have compiled the following list of organizations concerned with the issues debated in this book. The descriptions are derived from materials provided by the organizations. All have publications or information available for interested readers. The list was compiled on the date of publication of the present volume; names, addresses, phone and fax numbers, and e-mail and Internet addresses may change. Be aware that many organizations take several weeks or longer to respond to inquiries, so allow as much time as possible.

Advanced Cell Technology
One Innovation Dr., Biotech Three, Worcester, MA 01605
(508) 756-1212 • fax: (508) 756-4468
Web site: www.advancedcell.com

Advanced Cell Technology is a leading biotechnology company in the emerging field of regenerative medicine. Its focus is on cloning technology for the production of young cells for the treatment of cell degenerative diseases.

American Life League (ALL)
PO Box 1350, Stafford, VA 22555
(560) 659-4171 • fax: (540) 659-2586
e-mail: jbrown@all.org • Web site: www.all.org

ALL is an educational pro-life organization that opposes abortion, artificial contraception, reproductive technologies, and fetal experimentation. It asserts that it is immoral to perform experiments on living human embryos and fetuses, whether inside or outside the mother's womb. Its publications include the policy statement "Creating a Pro-Life America," the paper "What Is Norplant?," and the booklet *Contraceptive Compromise: The Perfect Crime.*

American Medical Association (AMA)
515 N. State St., Chicago, IL 60610
(800) 621-8335
Web site: www.ama-assn.org

The AMA is the largest and most prestigious professional association for medical doctors. It helps set standards for medical education and practices and is a powerful lobby in Washington for physicians' interests. The association publishes monthly journals for many medical fields as well as the weekly *JAMA.*

American Society of Law, Medicine, and Ethics (ASLME)
765 Commonwealth Ave., Suite 1634, Boston, MA 02215
(617) 262-4990 • fax: (617) 437-7596
Web site: www.aslme.org

The society's members include physicians, attorneys, health care administrators, and others interested in the relationship between law, medicine, and ethics. It takes no positions but acts as a forum for discussion of issues such as cloning. The organization has an information clearinghouse and a library. It publishes the quarterlies *American Journal of Law* and *Journal of Law, Medicine, and Ethics*, the periodic *ASLME Briefings*, and books.

BC Biotechnology Alliance (BCBA)
1122 Mainland St., #450, Vancouver, BC V6B 5L1 Canada
(604) 689-5602 • fax: (604) 689-5603
Web site: www.biotech.pc.ca

The BCBA is an association for producers and users of biotechnology. The alliance works to increase public awareness and understanding of biotechnology, including the awareness of its potential contributions to society. The alliance's publications include the bimonthly newsletter *Biofax* and the annual *Directory of BC Biotechnology Capabilities*.

The Center for Bioethics and Human Dignity
2065 Half Day Rd., Bannockburn, IL 60015
(847) 317-8180 • fax: (847) 317-8101
e-mail: info@cbhd.org • Web site: www.cbhd.org

The Center for Bioethics and Human Dignity exists to help individuals and organizations address the pressing bioethical challenges of our day, including genetic intervention and reproductive technologies.

Center for Biomedical Ethics
PO Box 33, UMHC, Minneapolis, MN 55455
(612) 625-4917

The center seeks to advance and disseminate knowledge concerning ethical issues in health care and the life sciences. It conducts original research, offers educational programs, fosters public discussion and debate, and assists in the formulation of public policy. The center publishes a quarterly newsletter and reading packets on specific topics, including fetal tissue research.

Center for Genetics and Society
436 14th St., Suite 1302, Oakland, CA 94612
(510) 625-0819 • fax: (510) 625-0874

The Center for Genetics and Society is a nonprofit information and public affairs organization working to encourage responsible uses and effective societal governance of the new human genetic and reproductive technologies.

Clone Rights United Front/Clone Rights Action Center
506 Hudson St., New York, NY 10014
(212) 255-1439 • fax: (212) 463-0435
e-mail: r.wicker@verizon.net • Web site: www.clonerights.org

The Clone Rights United Front began as a one-issue reproductive rights organization. It was organized to oppose legislation that would make cloning a human being a felony. It is dedicated to the principle that reproductive rights, including cloning, are guaranteed by the U.S. Constitution, and that each citizen has the right to decide if, when, and how to reproduce.

The Genetics and Public Policy Center
1717 Massachusetts Ave. NW, Suite 530, Washington, DC 20036
(202) 663-5971 • fax: (202) 663-5992
e-mail: inquiries@DNApolicy.org • Web site: www.DNApolicy.org

The Genetics and Public Policy Center was established to be an independent and objective source of credible information on genetic technologies and genetic policies for the public, media, and policy makers.

Genetics Society of America
9650 Rockville Pike, Bethesda, MD 20814
(301) 571-1825 • fax: (301) 530-7079
Web site: www.genetics-gsa.org

The society promotes professional cooperation among persons working in genetics and related sciences. It publishes the monthly journal *Genetics.*

The Hastings Center
21 Malcolm Gordon Rd., Garrison, NY 10524-5555
(845) 424-4040 • fax: (845) 424-4545
e-mail: mail@thehastingscenter.org
Web site: www.thehastingscenter.org

Since its founding in 1969, the Hastings Center has played a pivotal role in exploring the medical, ethical, and social ramifications of biomedical advances. The center publishes books, papers, guidelines, and the bimonthly *Hastings Center Report.*

Joseph and Rose Kennedy Institute of Ethics
Healy Hall, 4th Floor, Georgetown University, Washington, DC 20057
(202) 687-8099 • fax: (202) 687-8089
Web site: www.georgetown.edu

The institute sponsors research on medical ethics, including ethical issues surrounding the use of recombinant DNA and human gene therapy. It supplies the National Library of Medicine with an online database on bioethics and publishes an annual bibliography in addition to reports and articles on specific issues concerning medical ethics.

The Reprogen Organization
17 Gr. Xenopoulou St., Suite 2A, PO Box 53117, 3300 Limassol,
Cyprus
357-25-866300 • fax: 357-25-866301
e-mail: info@reprogen.org • Web site: www.reprogen.org

The Reprogen Organization is a center dedicated to the study of reproductive DNA cloning technology. It believes that the significant advances being made in reproductive cloning technology will afford an opportunity for those who are suffering from infertility to create a child of their own.

Bibliography

Books

Kenneth Alonso — *Shall We Clone a Man? Genetic Engineering and the Issues of Life: A View from a Catholic Physician Scientist*. Atlanta, GA: Allegro Press, 1999.

Lori B. Andrews — *The Clone Age: Adventures in the New World of Reproductive Technology*. New York: Henry Holt, 1999.

Ronald Cole-Turner — *Human Cloning: Religious Responses*. Louisville, KY: Westminster John Knox Press, 1997.

John Harris — *On Cloning*. London: Routledge, 2004.

Arlene Judith Klotzko — *The Cloning Sourcebook*. New York: Oxford University Press, 2001.

Paul Lauritzen — *Cloning and the Future of Human Embryo Research*. New York: Oxford University Press, 2001.

Lane P. Lester with James C. Hefley — *Human Cloning: Playing God or Scientific Progress?* Grand Rapids, MI: Fleming H. Revell, 1998.

Barbara MacKinnon — *Human Cloning: Science, Ethics, and Public Policy*. Urbana: University of Illinois Press, 2000.

Glenn McGee — *The Human Cloning Debate*. Berkeley, CA: Berkeley Hills Books, 2002.

Lee M. Silver — *Remaking Eden: Cloning and Beyond in a Brave New World*. New York: Avon Books, 1997.

Brent Waters and Ronald Cole-Turner — *God and the Embryo: Religious Voices on Stem Cells and Cloning*. Washington, DC: Georgetown University Press, 2003.

Periodicals

Ronald Bailey — "Is Brave New World Inevitable? Bill Kristol Says Yes. He's Wrong," *Reason*, April 24, 2002.

Russell Blackford — "Who's Afraid of the Brave New World," *Quadrant*, May 2003.

Barry L. Brown — "Human Cloning and Genetic Engineering: The Case for Proceeding Cautiously," *Albany Law Review*, Spring 2002.

Arthur L. Caplan — "Attack of the Anti-Cloners," *Nation*, June 17, 2002.

Eric Cohen and
William Kristol
"No, It's a Moral Monstrosity," *Human Life Review*,
Fall 2001.

Dinesh D'Souza
"Staying Human: The Danger of Techno-Utopia,"
National Review, January 22, 2001.

Elizabeth Price Foley
"Human Cloning and the Right to Reproduce,"
Albany Law Review, Spring 2002.

David van Gend
"The First Clone: Nobody's Child," *Human Life
Review*, Fall 2001.

Rudolf Jaenisch
and Ian Wilmut
"Don't Clone Humans!" *Science*, March 30, 2001.

Leon R. Kass
"Preventing a Brave New World," *Human Life
Review*, Summer 2001.

Leon R. Kass
"The Public's Stake," *Public Interest*, Winter 2003.

Charles Krauthammer
"Crossing Lines—A Secular Argument Against
Research Cloning," *New Republic*, April 29, 2002.

Chris Mooney
"The Future Is Later: The Cloning Fight Comes
Down to Abortion—and Down to Earth," *American
Prospect*, July 15, 2002.

Charles Murtaugh
"Shun Cloning: Scientists Must Speak Out," *Com-
monweal*, May 18, 2001.

Jeremy Rifkin
"Why I Oppose Human Cloning," *Tikkun*,
July/August 2002.

Diana Schaub
"Slavery Plus Abortion," *Public Interest*, Winter
2003.

Thomas A. Shannon
"The Rush to Clone: It Is Unethical to Apply This
Unproven Research to Humans," *America*, Septem-
ber 10, 2001.

Jenny Teichman
"The Grisly Science of Embryo Cloning," *New Cri-
terion*, June 2001.

James Q. Wilson
and Leon Kass
"The Ethics of Human Cloning," *American
Enterprise*, March 1999.

Internet Sources

George W. Bush
"Remarks by the President on Human Cloning
Legislation," White House, April 10, 2002. www.
whitehouse.gov.

Amy Coxon
"Therapeutic Cloning: An Oxymoron," Center for
Bioethics and Human Dignity, March 13, 2002.
www.cbhd.org.

U.S. Department
of Energy
"Cloning Fact Sheet," www.ornl.gov.

Index